# *Mindfulness*

## FOR

## SURVIVING LIFE'S CHALLENGES

# Mindfulness

## FOR
## SURVIVING LIFE'S CHALLENGES

### 50 MEDITATIONS TO GUIDE
### YOU TO PEACE

*Courtney Sunday*

Helios
press

*For Theo.*

*I would do it all again in a heartbeat just to meet you.*
*You make everything better.*

# Contents

# Foreword

**M**ake it stop. *Make it stop. Make it stop.*

For most of 2018, this was my mantra. I had given birth in late 2017 to the most delicious baby boy, a little being who blew my world open and made me eat my past words "When I'm a parent, I will . . ." because when you are in love you will do anything. You become stupid and you also become crystal clear.

During this year of baby bliss, I also had another companion: pain. Just before my son's birth, I started what I assumed was back labor. When the epidural wore off, the pain was almost worse than it was during eight centimeters. I had never given birth before, so I didn't know what was normal.

This certainly was not. After months of being told everything from the "fact" that it was my pelvic floor to the "fact" that it was in my head, the diagnosis was a herniated disc. So herniated that my disc didn't seem to know it belonged in any way to my spine. Nerves were compressed so dramatically I couldn't walk without a searing burning pain that was beyond anything I had ever known. At the age of thirty-seven, I found myself with a cane and a baby—two things I had never envisioned would coexist in my life.

Before birth, I was an active yoga teacher. After birth, I was so uncomfortable I couldn't slouch, lie down, or walk. I couldn't touch my knees, let alone my toes. I was in a bubble of love and a bubble of pain. I knew that life was composed of dramatic opposites, but living with them side by side was staggeringly complex. I went from feeling like I was in the best moment of my life to wondering if I could go on.

"When I'm a parent, I will travel the world with my little one. I will be active. I will be myself," I rattled off while I was pregnant. Pain made me realize that a lot of my super healthy, eat-avocado-toast-for-breakfast lifestyle habits had not made me as bulletproof as I had assumed. I was in a world that I had previously, secretly associated with being lazy. I stopped being physical with my partner because even a hug was painful. I stopped visiting my family because a car ride could mean a long stint of nerve pain.

I stopped.

Did I mention I had written a mindfulness book prior to this event? Being mindful, doing body scans, even breathing were real and sometimes impossible practices to me now. Breathing deeply *hurt*. I had to change my approach to life and I had to do it fast. I was getting grumpy. I was becoming unlikeable. I was telling my pain story over and over again because it felt like my whole world and because it felt like there was no way out.

This book is my attempt to share my struggle, to find peace, and to move forward. I dedicate this book to anyone who has pain that feels insurmountable. I dedicate this book to anyone who feels like the only one. Sometimes you will be in the dark for a long time. That is okay. Trust that there will be a light day in front of you.

If you can't trust, I will do it for you.

I practiced these mindfulness exercises on my very worst days. I came up with these meditations when I was sick and tired of feeling sick and tired. Every day when you are in pain has its own brand of challenging. I started asking myself to deal with each day in specific, measurable ways that I garnered from years of mindfulness practice.

I recently met a man in a playground (this was less creepy than it sounds) and he told me about how he had almost died a decade ago. He said "I wish I could have learned the lessons I now know without chemotherapy." Whether you have learned your own lessons because of chemotherapy, great loss, or the breaking of your heart is your journey. This book can be read linearly, but it was designed to be read in short bursts on your most difficult days. It can also be read in honor of someone that you love who is hurting.

My greatest hope is that one person who reads this book reads it at the right time. When you can't touch the sky (let's be honest, it's way up there), touch the ground. It's more than good enough when life is exhausting and messy. Use these exercises in the most uncomfortable, distressing, and painful times. Mindfulness is there to remind you that you have grit, you have an inner support system, and now you have this book to get you to wherever it is you need to get to.

I've got your back—even when mine is aching.

*—Courtney Sunday*

# *Mindfulness*
## FOR PAIN

There are moments in life when you want to curl up into a ball and hide under the covers. You assume they will pass, and they do, but they often come back. Some of us learn how to roll with the punches and manifest the line "This too shall pass." However, many of us get worse at encountering pain with time. We want it to be over, like, yesterday.

We like to measure our lives in all of the good: the degrees we have obtained, the ladders we have climbed, or the children we have raised. The times when we are on the couch or in the hospital bed or collapsed on the floor are not what we like to include as part of us. Yet, there they are. The exercises in this section are well suited for the times in your life when you wonder "What is the point?" and can't manage the basics or muster the joy.

When pain shows up and you are not having it, these mindfulness exercises will meet you where you are and offer suggestions for small ways to move forward. You are in the trenches, and trenches are notoriously muddy and uncomfortable. I don't expect you to reinvent your life right now, because if someone had suggested such a thing when I was on the floor, I would have unapologetically shown them the door.

A trench is a depression in the ground. Let's try to get to ground level together.

# Mindfulness

# Mindfulness

## FOR WHEN EVERYONE ELSE HAS IT BETTER THAN YOU

Ever looked at people and assumed you knew their story? If you have never done this, congratulations, you are better than me. If you have, welcome to the club of the not-so-perfect. While I started small, judging my inner landscape, eventually my full-blown judgment coughed its way out. I was judging other people for a whole host of things, from their etiquette to their parenting.

I was hurting on the inside and I wanted the rest of the world to hurt, too. Of course, when you are in this mindset, it is so difficult to see it. I only noticed when a friend said something so beautifully nonjudgmental about a topic many people would find easy to judge. It was such a simple statement but somehow magnified my own judgment. Her nonjudgment teased out what my mind had really been about, and it was only then that I saw it was ugly.

Have you ever been ugly on the inside?

If you haven't, first I will say to you, really? *Really*? Then I will ask to drink your Kool-Aid (even though I have stayed away from that product since the eighties). If you have been ugly, it is time to get all pretty again on the inside. Let's exorcise our ugly together. How do you do this? It's a lot harder than buying the right mascara, even though it sounds a heck of a lot easier.

Step one you have already completed. You have noticed the judgment cycle. This is a really big deal. You have stepped outside of a habit to see yourself more clearly, and this in itself is amazing. It's a little less amazing if you do nothing about it. (See? That was a little judgey. I obviously need to heed my own advice.)

The next step is to have a mantra that will help you remain accountable. When you are convinced someone has it better than you, that you know their own story, or you judge the ease or difficulty of their life, repeat your mantra. Some good examples are:

I wish this person health and happiness.

I release my judgment.

I accept who this person is at this moment.

Remember that this can be directed as much to yourself as to the troll on social media.

Judging is addictive and can be a tough cycle to break. In fact, it probably won't break completely because you are human. We all are, and won't morph into paradigms of perfection overnight, but we can all learn to be better and do better and let go of our own assumptions.

When you find yourself assuming, try reminding yourself that "I am making an assumption." Do you know for sure that someone hates you? Do you know for sure that they are talking behind your back? Do you know for sure that they think of you at all, or that they aren't in pain, too?

Food for thought.

# *Mindfulness*

## FOR WHEN YOU ARE AWAKE BECAUSE OF PAIN

There were months when I couldn't sleep more than forty-five minutes at a time. I did hypnotherapy, I meditated, cried, watched baking shows, listened to podcasts, fell asleep briefly for forty-five minutes, woke up in excruciating pain, fed my baby, and repeated. Repeating that cycle for one night is exhausting in itself. Repeating it for months made me sort of crazy. Maybe even totally crazy, but I was postpartum, so I am going to cut myself a break.

It's always best to cut postpartum women a break.

The thing about going through a period of sleep deprivation is that you will not become better for it. There are many things that we can push through or reframe, but not getting something as essential as sleep shatters any facade of "I'm okay." I had no shield. In retrospect, I feel for the innocent strangers who asked me how I was doing. (Cue a monstrosity of emotion.)

Why the heck am I writing about something I didn't do a good job of mastering? Because at the time I was frantically searching for someone like me who got it. Someone who understood that pain can keep us up, make us crazy, and be too much to rise above. There is no phoenix in sleep deprivation. I've looked. So, if this is you, up in the middle of the night with pain, I get it. And it turns out there are others who do, too. There is an army of people who hurt. There are people like you who can't at all remember what it feels like to be well rested.

You are not alone.

Even when the road ahead is uncertain, meditation is one way to connect everything around you, to keep you from feeling fragmented. It is not you and your pain versus the rest of the world. You are still a part of the continuum. You still have a pulse in this heartbeat of life.

One of the most profound spiritual experiences happened for me (stereotypically) in Bali. I was advised to practice "noble silence," not talking to anyone or engaging with anything distracting like a phone or even a book. After weeks of meditating, I had a quick glimpse of continuity. I opened my eyes to a sunrise and I could see and feel that everything is connected. Where I was then, where I was before, everyone I knew, and everyone I didn't—it was all linked—and it all seemed so simple.

Like any glimpse, this didn't last, but I do remember it. It was key that I remembered it when I began mentally healing, which happened far before I did physically. I was on the road to depression and the only way out was to forge a spiritual community. It started with a community of one, because in the beginning there was no way I was reaching out or meeting new people. That felt daunting. However, I could take a step outside of the pity bubble, especially when I had so many wakeful hours. I could choose to spend most of those hours wallowing, but I didn't have to spend *all* of the time consumed by my dejection, so I started sending out healing to anyone else with back pain. When I woke up, I gave a part of my energy to those other silent, unknown, suffering people. More than anything (even more than baking shows) this helped. I felt calmer. I felt part of a bigger circle. I sometimes could even sleep for more than an hour. It gave me something to do other than master my melancholy.

When you are awake because of pain, what fraction of your energy can you dedicate to something other than woe? Even 1 percent is better than 0. Tiny, baby steps are all we can ask of ourselves in challenging times. Those baby steps can eventually walk us toward something that looks like regeneration.

# *Mindfulness*
## FOR WHEN YOUR WHOLE LIFE HAS TURNED UPSIDE DOWN

**M**any of us have had a moment in the middle of the night when we've been concerned that everything was going to change. Whether it is a job loss, a breakup, or just plain worry, our minds are adept at keeping us up. We all have a threshold for how much pain or change we can endure. When it hits the upper limit, we may feel like we are going to crack.

I knew my whole life had turned upside down in the middle of a conversation with a friend. She was taking about a new fling and I found myself drifting away. I was so caught up in my difficulties that I couldn't focus on her story. Frankly, her story seemed trivial.

If your relationship has ever been on the brink, you know this feeling. A fight has crossed a line. You realize that this may be the beginning of the end. You immediately start making plans (and it always feels like those plans have to be made in the middle of the night), but when your whole life has turned upside down, you need to stop with the plans.

I'm serious.

It is enough that there is so much change. It is enough that things are difficult. Trying to make things work or fix things isn't actually doing much (besides sending you into a downward trajectory). It is best to stay put, to not map out your new life when you feel this way. *Feeling* is exhausting enough.

One thing I thought to myself when I was feeling like there was no continuity in my world from the past and my world in the present was *this is only temporary*. Mantra:

This is only temporary.

This is only temporary.

This is *only* temporary.

Did I believe it the more I said it? Hell, no. (At least, not right away.) Why bother, you may wonder? Because although I couldn't promise myself that I was going to return to my old perky self, I could promise myself that I would not stay stagnant. My life has been many things, but predictable is not one of them.

I suspect your life is pretty similar.

Somehow, we treat pain differently from pleasure. We think it will stick. Pain may live alongside you, but it won't stay the same. It will shift. It is not permanent, because nothing about you is and ever has been. I can't promise you that you will feel amazing tomorrow, but I can promise you that today is not every day.

Say it with me: "This is only temporary." Eventually, one day, you will believe it. You may just have to get through a few months of your own eye-rolling to get there.

# Mindfulness

## FOR WHEN YOU GET BETTER
## (AND ARE AFRAID OF GETTING WORSE)

People's favorite thing to say to someone going through a rough time (whether physically or mentally) is "It will get better." There are a host of clichés that apply here: "Tomorrow is a new day," or "Take it one step at a time." Some of them are true. Some of them make you want to lash out and say "How do you know?"

Speaking with a family friend about his chronic pain, which he hadn't had for five years, he said he still lived in fear every day. Five years is a lot of fear. His fear limited the movements he made, how he slept, and even the activities he decided to do.

Getting out of physical pain is one thing. Getting over the experience is a whole different ballgame. Like with grief, we can't expect to ever get "over" a loss. We readjust our lives, we find other spaces inside of ourselves and, ultimately, we accept that there may be a little sadness. Always. Forever. When there is physical pain or illness that has taken over your life for some time, it is hard to be the same afterward, even if the pain dissipates. You may move differently. You may never feel as carefree. There is an inherent nervousness.

I found most books about pain annoyingly optimistic when I was in the throes of difficulty. Authors tried to promise a light at the end of the tunnel, when, really, there was no way they could promise their readers that their chronic pain or condition would go away. I found myself closing book after book, wondering if my frustration was a character flaw or if others felt this way, too.

I was annoyed with myself, especially when I became reinjured, but I was more annoyed at the world.

*I was a good person! I didn't deserve this!* my inner monologue would declare, until I realized, *who* did *deserve this?* I am no different from anyone else experiencing adversity or having difficulty. I am a human being and sometimes a human being feels awful. I started remembering what a physical therapist had told me months ago: "This is going to take time."

Of course, I promptly ignored her because I felt that my sheer determination, fitness level, and healthy diet would make me different.

It didn't.

"This is going to take time." Patience is so difficult when it comes to our own selves. I have endless patience for my son but so little for myself. When you find yourself frightened about getting worse, frightened about the future, and willing to change your lifestyle so that pain is at the forefront, please take a deep breath. Remind yourself, "This is going to take time." Admit and breathe into the fear rather than ignoring it because ignored emotions are just going to grow with time.

You may get better. You may get worse. I don't know your story, your personality, your body, but I do know that the pain has won when you decide to live a contracted life. Do what you can do and don't force the rest until it is ready to come. Some days I would sit in a rigid robotic position and that was it. Some days I would read books and ignore text messages because it was too much work to lie and tell people that I was getting better just because it felt like that was all they wanted to hear.

When I woke up, I started to do something different from checking my phone, running on autopilot, or feeding my negativity. I let myself pause to see what I needed. I let myself feel sad and angry and disappointed and grateful. You can feel all of these things at once because living as a human being is a full, exhaustive experience.

You are probably reading this book because you can't do as much as you used to. You can, however, feel even more. You can give yourself permission to feel something, whatever that something needs to be for you today.

Even if just for a moment, have gratitude for that something. Gratitude will fill your body with more than the stress hormones that have been taking over. Gratitude may remind you that even in the hardest of times, there is resilience.

There is peace.

# *Mindfulness*
## FOR WHEN YOUR HOPE IS GONE

I am seen as a relentlessly positive person. Note the word relentless. I have evidence. There are photos that have been taken of me during times of my life where I was crumbling on the inside. Somehow, I still looked happy.

Always-smiling people are not the best at being vulnerable.

I wasn't even intentionally faking it. If you took all the days of my life thus far, I wouldn't be surprised to see that there have been more happy days than sad days. Perhaps in the throes of sadness, my face simply didn't know what to do with itself.

When I was in excruciating pain for so long, I stopped looking at my future. My family would talk about my future in the way that people do when they are desperately trying to cheer someone up. They would describe the future as if they could see it. It was shiny and pretty. In this future, I was not in pain. I was in love with my life.

In their fairytale version, things worked out. In my head, they did not.

Sometimes I would listen to their attempts to fix the situation and I would say nothing. Other times I would argue with them as the voice of despair battling against the voice of hope. I didn't have hope. I had an everyday routine, where I would get to the end of the day without triumph. There was just another day to be lived trying to get out of bed, brush my teeth, care for my family, and feed myself.

I know from being candid with my friends and even from acquaintances that have suffered deep, true, meaningful pain that I was not the only one on the planet who didn't have a relationship with hope. No-hope-land is a very difficult place to live. It is another point of life's journey that is solitary.

I have a lot of friends and a loving family. But I had no choice but to be hopeless alone. If you are feeling similarly, I am not here to tell you to breathe better or to drink more kombucha or to say affirmations in the shower. I am telling you that to be mindful is to be hopeful for hope itself. It is to recognize that this is a moment (and a shitty moment at that) but it is not every moment.

Our minds can inform us that we are indeed going to get way better or they can inform us that this is the end of our good days. Neither one is necessarily true. When you are panicked, when your hope is lost, remind yourself that today is today. It is not a prediction of tomorrow or next week or next year.

If you have the space in your hopelessness, you can tell yourself this exact thing: "Today is today." This is not my truth, it is just *the* truth. If you can walk, you can remind yourself, simply, to put one foot in front of the other. And every time your mind convinces you that it can zoom into the future and let you know what is on the horizon, politely but firmly decline.

It's one step. It's one day. It's the hope for hope.

# *Mindfulness*

## FOR WHEN YOU CAN'T FIND THE OLD VERSION OF YOURSELF

Recently, I heard a woman in a cafe say something cruel about someone she was dating. I cringed, and truly, it was a two-part cringe. Hearing cruelty out loud doesn't put a good taste in any of our mouths, but I was also cringing because I had *been* that woman.

I used to desperately want to prove in every relationship that I was independent and untethered to love. Sometimes my actions didn't come close to backing this up. When I found myself in a moment of dissonance, I would become a little mean. I would justify this behavior, of course, because sometimes we justify our behavior even when we internally know it is wrong.

But I did it.

I also did other deplorable things in my past that involved hurting people. I've been unkind. We probably all have, but it is hard to write that because I would like you to believe that I am always, and always have been, nice.

There you go. My nasty, on a silver platter.

If you were to meet me ten years ago, old me had nicer skin, a greater supply of energy, and an impressive tolerance for tequila (we all have our strengths). If you met me now, new me is softer, a little more introspective, and someone who works to tame my bad qualities. Even this new me is not a steady thing. I could go back to old me, although probably with older skin because this mama is not getting her beauty rest.

This is a roundabout way of letting you know that if you, like me, are begrudging who you are in exchange for who you used to be, the story isn't entirely linear. Sure, I had a body that could do six hours of yoga, a spin class, and eat a buffet dinner, but I didn't have the ability to spot a true friend. In the past, I could relax into hypermobile yoga poses while now I can relax into strong and difficult feelings.

We don't get to become better versions of ourselves for free. This doesn't mean that I am rationalizing your difficulty. I would never dare do such a thing. However, it does mean that we can't just wish away the present. I found myself thinking of the graduation speech "Everybody's Free," released as a song by Baz Luhrmann in 1998:

"Advice is a form of nostalgia

Dispensing it is a way of fishing the past from the disposal, wiping it off

painting over the ugly parts and recycling it for more than it's worth."

The older I get, the more I realize that graduation speeches are really for the parents of the graduates. For most of us, these speeches are far too nuanced to fully absorb at twenty-two.

Pain can also bring us into nostalgia, "painting over the ugly parts and recycling it for more than it's worth." Just because you weren't in this much pain before doesn't mean that you were absolutely spectacular either. You may not have had this discomfort, but that doesn't mean that you were your best self. (Or maybe you were. I don't know your story.) Nostalgia is also a fancy way of letting you know that your mind is getting stuck on a loop that is firmly entrenched in the past. The only way out is by learning to refocus your attention.

Try this five-senses mindfulness exercise, which is as simple as it sounds. Give each sense a minute of your time. The order does not matter.

Hear the sounds around you.

Smell your environment.

See your surroundings.

Taste, even the aftertaste of a meal (I prefer chocolate.).

Notice the contact of touch—the floor, your clothing, the temperature of your body.

When you are done, pause. It's all about the pause.

There really was no old you. There is only present you. You just need five minutes to remember that.

# *Mindfulness*

## FOR WHEN YOU FEEL ISOLATED

I have friends who have gone radio silent for long periods of time. Life gets busy. It's easy to get swept up in our own lives and to take social media as the truth. I now realize that if it has been a really long time since I have talked to a true friend, it is likely because one of us is going through a hard time.

It's so easy to think that we are burdening people when we are in a negative place. The North American reply to "How are you?" is "Fine." Even if we aren't fine, we're conditioned to just say "fine," smile, and get on with it. Culturally, we take this as very normal. This must be confusing for people learning English as a second language.

We have not made much room for the world outside of "fine," which is a world all of us inhabit at one time or another. While the rare person tells the truth of a not-so-fine day on social media, the majority of these applications are designed to focus on the positive, filter out the negative, and simplify the human experience in a hashtag.

It is no wonder that when feelings become frustrating, difficult, or painful, we don't quite know what to do with them. My most painful days meant that walking around the block was serious work. It was harder work than when I ran a half marathon in a body that felt young and capable. I would slowly shuffle, and every moment of every step felt like my body was saying "no." The whole experience of "yes" had to come from my mind, yet when someone asked me "How are you?" I would say "Fine."

Fine. The biggest bold-faced lie of our time.

This behavior made me feel more and more isolated. I started distancing myself and comparing myself to others constantly. I would pass a mother with a jogging stroller and wonder what it would be like to both have a baby and be able to move. I would be struck by jealousy of strangers, such as a woman sitting in a café licking cappuccino milk off of her spoon. I would imagine this stranger's life in great detail, someone who certainly, definitely did not have the pain that I was having.

Something fascinating happened to me when my son was four months old. I was having a good week, able to walk for more than ten minutes at a time. A stranger stopped to coo at our baby. As all parents do, we thought he was the most beautiful and clever boy that had ever lived. (He still is, by the way. I'm not biased at all.) We soaked up her praise and then as she left, she said "What a perfect family. I'm jealous."

*Jealous?*

I was sleeping on the floor and had to psych myself up to stand for night feedings. I ate a bowl of cereal for lunch because I wasn't strong enough to make anything else. I was dividing my life into "before" and "after" pain. Her comment drew out an epiphany.

*People can't see my pain.*

The most obvious truths can get foggy when life is difficult. I was limping, and people saw my smile. I was wincing, and people saw my sweet baby. I was short of breath, and they were too busy processing their own days to notice.

People close to me could tell the difference, but there was a whole world who had no idea that this was not me. They might see the young and capable mother that I had seen with the jogging stroller. They might think that I had it easy or that I had a charmed life.

Let this sink in: most people cannot see your pain.

The reason this statement matters is that it is equally true in reverse. You cannot see anyone else's pain. You are not the only one wandering around in a bubble of difficulty, finding it hard to move forward. You may notice a grieving friend's sarcasm while she masks her dark circles with concealer. A coworker may wince when opening a can of sparkling water, but you are too busy consuming your own to notice.

There is a world underneath the world of "fine."

This revelation was key in my mindfulness journey. I realized that I could use my experience as an injured person to expand my compassion rather than shirking in my isolation. I could use my pain as a way to see the world differently. The man walking down the street with a cane was now a warrior. The woman who was always running late was doing her best.

And gosh darn it, I was not alone.

*I am not the only one*, I would remind myself when my back would flare, and my world would seem as if it were contracting. I would silently send love to the people I didn't even know who were going through the exact same thing right at the same moment. I imagined us together and would sometimes even go through a metta meditation for me and these strangers: "May we find peace. May we be happy. May we find love." The meditation is often done with the word "health," but on my worst days, that felt like too big of an ask. We can all rewrite it as needed.

What do you wish for yourself? What do you wish a stranger saw in you? What can you give the world that you wish it was giving you? The more we feel for others, the better we feel. It doesn't mean all of our pain will go away, but it does mean that it will take us out of our isolation, offering a different view of the world.

# *Mindfulness*

I don't have a great sense of direction.

There, I said it.

A lack of an internal compass has not kept me from exploring. In fact, for a time, I had more stamps on my passport than most people I knew. Still, I got lost in many different languages. I once dropped my backpack off at a hostel in Paris and couldn't find my way back to it (which was fine, as it was fortuitously La Nuit des Musées, an annual celebration in which museums are free and open until midnight). Although I can see the blessings in my geographic misfortunes, I couldn't quite find the blessings when I felt deeply, irrevocably lost within myself.

Whether we have physical pain or not, life hits us in the face from time to time. We suffer. It wasn't until I felt myself identify more with this suffering than any other facet of myself that I realized it was time to get reoriented.

I needed to find my map.

My pain was so bone deep that I couldn't ignore the waves of agony. However, underneath the pain was a secondary suffering. In this layer, there was anxiety and resentment that walked alongside my pain and difficulty. I needed to learn how to work with my thoughts and emotions rather than identifying myself with every thought that came into my mind. Without doing this, every negative thought, from the "I'm not going to get better ever" variety to the "there will be no more pleasure in life" kinds were weighing me down and sweeping me away.

Every thought has an attitude. When you cover the nature of your thoughts, you can categorize, the way Marie Kondo might do. (That woman can organize anything.) "This is an angry thought." "This is a bitter thought." "This is a dejected thought." We are not going to erase our thoughts, but with training, we can let go of the hardening that happens around pain. We can experience what is, without expanding from primary pain into secondary and perhaps even tertiary pain.

Every single time we feel lost, there is a glimmer of hope. You have noticed that you have felt lost. In that very act of noticing, you can choose differently. (When traveling, this is when I rely on the kindness of strangers. Or a GPS.) In times of great strife, you may feel that the logical choice is to stay put and focus on your pain. There is absolutely nothing wrong with that. You aren't a robot. However, at other times you may wish to open up two dimensions. In one dimension is the fatigue, the discomfort, the difficulty. The second dimension is cocooned around the pain: the rest of life. The rest of life may include a warm cup of tea, a sweet hug from a child, a mesmerizing book.

There is more to life than our pain and difficulty, even when it feels like it is everything. With fine tuning, you may find that underneath the most laborious of breaths is a deep well of love, compassion, and curiosity.

We can get out our compass. We can read our map. We can find our way home. The next time you feel lost, enter the portal of mindfulness. With a trained mind, your mindfulness can create magic.

# *Mindfulness*
## FOR WHEN YOU DON'T RECOGNIZE YOURSELF ANYMORE

When I started telling people I was writing this book, I received stories in return. It was as if I gave strangers permission to bypass the small talk. Pain *is* deep conversation. (No one really misses the conversations about weather, anyway.)

During one of these conversations—while I was wearing a sparkly candy cane Christmas dress, by the way, which is an important detail because the dress clashed with the conversation—I listened to a story of not being heard. A woman's story of being afraid to admit pain because of what it could do professionally and personally, especially because she was told it was all in her head. "I was under a lot of stress, so that may have been partially true," she told me. "But it was not the whole story." The whole story is an important one if you have had a profound, lasting, chronic pain experience. It changes how you treat the rest of the world. It changes how you view yourself. If anyone discounts this, whether it is a doctor or a family member, it may feel as if they are discounting who you are at the core.

Although we aren't our pain (and mindfulness helps us realize that), we are different because of it. Sometimes it makes us better, and it makes our compassion bloom. At other times, it makes us worse, and makes the rest of the world's problems seem immaterial. When you don't recognize yourself anymore, chances are that you have identified too strongly with the pain. It has become you and enveloped you. Mindfulness gives that pain a place. It recognizes it so that it doesn't feel the need to shout.

This woman I spoke to in my obnoxiously sparkly dress told me what helped her. It was a laundry list of things, because we all find out eventually what magic works for us. Her magic was opera. She listened to it and was moved. Feeling art is powerful. It's amazing that even for a few moments, it can make someone suffer just a little less. If you haven't seen yourself in some time, go find your version of opera. It may be classic rock. It may be the sound of a purring cat. It may be a poster that you used to have on your college dorm wall that brings good memories. (Bob Marley and Miles Davis, I am talking to you.)

Reconnect with yourself through something that relaxes you, or on your worst days, something that used to relax you. Commit to it as a practice. It wasn't until I lost my mobility that I finally, *finally* understood the idea of yoga and meditation as a practice. I wasn't going to get more advanced ad infinitum, so I opened myself up more to the full experience of being human, warts and all, and practiced being Courtney a little more—every single day.

Find your opera. Find yourself. You're in there somewhere, I promise.

# Mindfulness

## FOR WHEN THERE IS NO COMFORTABLE POSITION

I feel embarrassed that I used to teach yoga classes that began with "assume a comfortable position." I would then proceed to dictate what it meant to be "comfortable." The sitting bones were level. The spine was upright, but not rigid. The shoulders were aligned over the hips. Hips sinking into the ground.

*Cringe.*

Once I got an injury in which there was literally no comfortable position, this version of myself made me blush. I was excluding the people whose backs hurt, whose knees troubled them, or who were just plain inflexible. I was excluding in the name of everyone coming together. I thought I was finding *the* comfortable position. It took my reality check to realize: there is no position that will ever work for everyone, no matter how many bolsters and blocks and supports I may offer those people.

My own words kept ringing in my ears when I was faced with the conundrum of no comfortable position. I couldn't lie down on either side, on my belly, or my back. I couldn't sit for too long. Standing was excruciating. How was I supposed to find the peace when I could not find the comfort?

It wasn't easy.

Many days I was so annoyed with my condition that I got annoyed at my partner, because he was there (poor guy). He would tell me I had already told him the story of my uncomfortable body, and I would lash out, telling him he should hear it again. He had the body that worked so he should know what it was like to have a body that didn't. My anger was real, and it certainly wasn't helping, so I started giving myself different directions. If there was no comfortable seat, could I make myself 10 percent more comfortable with the uncomfortable seat? Ten percent seemed doable. Sometimes it meant simply moving my leg a little more to the right or letting my toes relax. It didn't bring a sense of relief akin to a body that was pain free, but it did feel oddly relieving to know that I still had some say.

When your body doesn't feel like it is working, do your best to find this 10 percent. Sometimes this is as simple as taking a moment to notice where you are contracted. When I was in extreme pain, I felt it everywhere: my shoulders, my back, my ankles, my feet. The old yoga teacher in me wanted to do a body scan where I could let the whole body go, but, frankly, that was just too big of a job.

However, I could relax my toes. I would do that until the pain would remind me of its presence. I didn't need to relax the whole body—I did what I could. This was a reminder that even though I wasn't comfortable, I was also not destined to be at maximum discomfort.

Relax what you can (including on an emotional level). Notice what you can't. We want to force our bodies to be better when they need us to be still. Pain is a message asking us to listen, and if we refuse, it can get louder. Listen to your pain. Let it be there, without allowing it to become your leader. And if this doesn't work tonight or tomorrow, don't give up. Your mind is doing the best that it can. Your body is working hard. There will be another day to try.

# *Mindfulness*
## FOR WHEN YOU WONDER HOW LONG
## THIS IS GOING TO TAKE

I'm going to write something difficult. My pain was so bad that at one point I couldn't imagine enjoying my own life again. I was going to be there for my son and enjoy watching him grow bigger and brighter, but I couldn't be there for myself.

If deep or chronic pain walks beside you every second, life might feel like it is out of your control. It is so easy to miss the magic of the first snowfall or the tenderness in your friend's eyes. It is so easy to be all body, no soul.

In one of my worst weeks, I mentally willed myself to get out of the house every single day. If it had just been me, I would have wallowed, but I had another person to impress and show the world to. My baby boy was fantastic at seeing joy in the small things, and I feigned contagion. We looked at trees, at grass, at dogs. He smiled at me like I was beautiful. His new eyes looked at me like I was whole.

I felt like neither.

On one of these walks, I ran into a former yoga student of mine. "When are we going to resume yoga classes?" she asked me, oblivious to my grimace as I sat down. "Oh, I need to take some time after the birth of this one," I said, gesturing to my kicking baby. She nodded and wished me well., and I realized I was feeling the pressure of the world to be better than I had been before. Women can have a traumatic birth, yet language is so skewed toward "bouncing back." It can be hard for any of us to process the dichotomy of who we were before and who we are now.

The world swirls around us and it begs us to stay the same. When you wonder how long this whole process is going to take, it is worth looking into the fact that you don't wonder how long your birthday is going to take. We have many things in life that, joyful or not, have an expiration date. Heck, *we* have expiration dates. We want to know our own story before it has been written. Pain, especially, is so immediate, so drenched in now-ness that it is difficult not to beg the future to unmask itself. There is no doctor, no psychic, no best friend who has the answer for your healing journey. Many people will give estimates, and if you would like, you can average them out until you feel a prophecy. Or you can give your body and mind a break.

It starts with stopping the speculation, and, man, do I know this is hard. Your mind will keep wondering, but you can stop feeding it by ceasing the conversations that are solution-less. The ones where you say the same story, and you get the same sympathy, and everyone goes around the suffering merry-go-round.

Then—and this is easy to write but harder to practice—do your best to stop waiting for the joy to come, or the pain to cease. This doesn't mean that you aren't allowing room for mending. Rather, you are increasing your tolerance for difficult situations. There is room for discomfort, even when it feels like you are giving in. You are working on finding room for torment or space for irritation. Doing this instead of focusing on an imaginary end date of suffering can help you move forward, one moment at a time.

For me, it was one walk, one smile, one shower, one well-deserved nap at a time. Eventually I realized that I had made room for a new version of myself, with less ego and more benevolence. This woman didn't care if she could do the splits or if she stood up differently. She was better at loving. She was stronger in different, quieter ways.

This process will take as long as it wants. You have some time to meet a new version of yourself.

# *Mindfulness*

## FOR WHEN BREATHING IS HARD

There were years of my life when I was pretty obsessed with breathing. I went to breathing workshops. I reminded people daily of the power of a deep breath. In a world of complexity and turmoil, breathing seemed like the one thing that made sense. When I was stressed or closed off my breathing would change, but if I paid attention to it, my inner world would simplify and transform, until my injury made it so that taking a deep breath was absolutely excruciating. Ever the fixer, I signed up for pain management courses, hired a coach, and read books about pain. Guess what everyone reminded me to do? Breathe.

*Thanks, everyone.*

Breathing in a mindful way wasn't working for me. With the position of my herniated disc and where my diaphragm (the primary breathing muscle) was located, my old ways of meditating were suddenly not working.

Years ago, I had a yoga student who suffered from trauma. She taught me that a deep breath can stir up emotions and scratch old wounds. Although breathing was a safe haven for me, life was never going to be simple enough to allow breath to mutate all difficulty.

Darn.

A lot of yoga explores the tug between desire and aversion. We sometimes spend a lot of day in desire, both on and off the mat. I love brownies, headstands, and cookbooks. Therefore, my inclination is to go toward those things as often as I can. Desire feels good momentarily but can be hard to temper and keep me from progressing. Then there are things I avoid, like negative people, soda, and pull-ups (the exercise, not the diaper, although admittedly I avoid both). While avoiding feels good, it doesn't teach me or challenge me.

It's not as if I am suggesting that spiritual mastery will squash all desire and aversion. It may simply make us aware of the fact that both of these aspects exist in all of us. When unwell, I desired a deep breath so badly. At first, I avoided learning new ways to cope. I wasn't helping myself, even though on the surface I felt like I was staying safe.

We have the aggravating ability to get in the way of our own peace. Whether or not you can take a deep breath, do a handstand, or even eat a brownie does not define you as a person. The world is not keeping score. By staying at arm's length from things and pulling the same things closer, you are keeping yourself from growing. If you are in pain, it is also keeping you from progressing.

A mindfulness exercise is to notice how you attach to the ideas of aversion and attraction. What are you crawling more toward at this point (ice cream, binge watching, online shopping)? What are you retreating from (intimacy, quiet time, friendships)? Can you take a step back from feeding the pain to notice how you react in this new (and admittedly crappy) circumstance?

Unhooking ourselves from these ways of thinking, according to Buddhists, will free us. You have the capacity to suffer less simply by engaging less with the drama of your mind. Try it just for today. You can always go back to that plate of brownies tomorrow.

# *Mindfulness*

## FOR WHEN YOU ARE STARVED FOR SPIRITUALITY

"It's in God's plan." When someone says that to you, do you feel comforted? Or diminished?

Years ago, I interviewed a young widow who had been deliriously in love and had one of those weddings that sparked jealousy. Then, her husband got cancer and died very soon after. For months, people did what people do when someone is grieving. They brought meals. They said things ranging from "I don't know what to say" to "God works in mysterious ways." The more people tried to justify the experience, the worse she felt. *Sure, there may be a plan,* she thought, *but that doesn't make my sorrow less.* Few people held space for her sadness. Few people seemed to get that there were no words that could make it all better. Her healing couldn't be talked away.

Recently, a friend of mine asked how I started my own mindful quest. I told her about a time I was achingly alone. The kind of alone that takes up every nook and cranny. The kind of alone that only goes away with some reconfiguration. I felt I had no choice but to reconfigure. I learned how to sit still, how to call myself on my own shit, and how to bravely hold space for myself. I learned how to be quiet. I learned how to forgive. I even found God.

Now, God to me is an evolving concept. God became my own; a notion so big I couldn't contain it. The idea of God was in me and in everything I did and it was what made me feel connected. I needed to ditch the religion I grew up with to find that spiritual connection.

If you are starved for spirituality in the midst of your deepest struggle, you are not alone. You may have looked in books and in temples, in classes and in prayer. You may assume that because you have been granted this moment of pain and misfortune, that there is no higher power. Or you may ask your higher power why you have been given this challenge.

Mindfulness doesn't always give us answers, but it does give us some semblance of peace. Spirituality can work much the same way. Being down and out is an opportunity to communicate to an unconditional power. We can find meaty goodness in the midst of everything that is trying to break us down.

Being broken open doesn't feel good but it can help eradicate the ego. The less we are attached to who we are and who we used to be, the more we can allow room for a new vibration. A new source. Maybe even God. This is not a single sentence or a single moment. This is life's work. A place to start is with whatever is good inside of you. See if you can take a moment to find it, to feel it, and maybe to share it with other people. Try it today. Then try again tomorrow.

The practice of mindfulness reminds us that we are magnificent (yes, even now), and finding your own magnificence can help build up our empathy. The one thing I know for sure about your future is that you will meet people who are suffering. When you encounter someone who is stumbling, inner spiritual work can keep you from glossing over the problems of others and will allow you to listen and be still with people in their hardest moments. You are probably still now more than ever. You are probably uncomfortable. What better time than now to begin?

# *Mindfulness*
## FOR WHEN YOU GET BAD NEWS

H ave you ever realized how many voices are in your head at any given time?

I speak particularly about the bad news voices. The voices of people who may have told you that you aren't good enough and that you aren't capable of change. The serious stuff that is hard to shake off, no matter how centered you are.

During the worst point of my injury, I met with many doctors. Surgeons. Specialists. Specialized specialists who were declared to be "the best" at what they do. These doctors walked into rooms with white coats and swagger. They were used to getting results, and I was suddenly another potential story to add to one of their academic papers. Many of these doctors were surprised by me. I was young. Fit. Not overweight. I had great posture. I wasn't the norm when it came to a back injury. However, they were used to having answers because people go to doctors with questions and hope to get at least some of them answered. New job description for physicians: question answerer.

Going to all of these appointments, I had no idea that I was welcoming some of these doctors' voices to start living in my head. They would say hopeful things, but it was the dramatic things that stuck. The dramatic thoughts were like chewing gum, my brain a shoe. I just couldn't scrape them off.

During one appointment, I was greeted by a doctor who was initially calming and pleasant. He said I would be feeling better soon after a spinal injection. He even said he was excited for me to feel better. How sweet was that? Then, he looked at an MRI of my spine and said matter-of-factly, "Even with surgery, the most you will have is ten years without extreme discomfort."

*Excuse me?*

From that moment on, whenever my pain flared up, whenever I had hard days, and whenever I doubted myself, I heard his voice. It rang and rang in my head. He also said I would never get better without surgery.

I got better without surgery and *still* I couldn't stop hearing his voice. Ten years. Ten years. *Ten years.* I felt like a giant human clock, wondering when my time would be up.

Healthcare professionals are human beings, and like every other human being, they get tired. They don't always review what they are going to say. Their compassion falters. They see patients and not people. That day, I was most definitely a patient, and my bright future felt like it was rapidly dimming. If you have recently received bad news, no matter what it happens to be, the mindfulness trick is to notice when you hear someone else's voice in your head. Are you listening to their statistics and prognosis rather than your individuality and capability? Are you letting the bad news story become your entire story?

To dig your way out, you must sit in the discomfort. Sit with the anger and the worry and the frustration. But let all of that be yours.

You don't have to carry someone else's opinion of how you will heal and how you will cope. This is a time to know yourself. The more you sit, the more your own voice will have the potential to emerge. At the very least, you will notice when you have a mantra, like *ten years* (which is an opinion, and not the truth, by the way). Doctor, thank you for your opinion. But I am more than my MRI. Bad news exists. Mindfulness is a practice designed not to make it worse.

# *Mindfulness*

## FOR WHEN IT'S ALL TOO MUCH

It wasn't until I had my son that I became aware of all of the reasons people could be kept awake at night. There is the glaringly obvious one of worry. I come from a long line of worriers, and from time to time, I find myself caught up in the genetic loop. Worry may start with deadlines and then end up somewhere entirely unrelated such as the issue of greenhouse gases.

Worry at night is powerful, and when you are in pain it can quadruple. There is something about the silence of a home that allows the mind to fester. In the darkness, all of the distractions shrink, and worry gets ample opportunity to magnify. Parenting made my worry grow because I didn't have much quiet time. Nap times were spent cleaning up, writing articles, or making my son's next meal. Parenting made me fall so madly in love that my heart teetered between broken and full most moments of the day. I was exhausted but not officially allowed to be. I didn't want to miss a moment. I didn't want to give up my identity, my work, my friends. Something had to give, and for me it was the precious sleep that I had so taken for granted.

When it's all too much, it is even more crucial to find time during the day to allow yourself to feel. A time when you are not a task-completing robot whizzing through the checklist of life.

We all need to find a little bit of slow.

The slow integrates the experience of pain, unlocking sadness if sadness is what is there. In the slow, we can remind ourselves that we are human and maybe even forgive ourselves for all of the things we didn't do right. On one day, perhaps my son's diet was not ideally balanced. On another day, perhaps I didn't perfect my physical therapy tasks. I have to go slow to remember that it all goes so fast, even the bad stuff that feels like it will last forever.

A meditation that helped me fall asleep when my mind was buzzing and clicking was the simple mantra, "I allow."

I allow myself to feel shitty and to not feel like I need to pretend otherwise.

I allow myself to feel overwhelmed.

I allow myself to be scared—of sleep deprivation, of love, of the future.

I allow myself to make mistakes without needing to explain to myself how I could have lived my life differently.

I allow.

I allow.

The state of allowing is powerful, because we can spend so much time in the alternate state of pretending that we have it all together and that we don't need space.

In pain or not, I'll bet you can benefit from some intentional space. To feel. To let go.

# *Mindfulness*

## FOR WHEN YOU WANT ANSWERS

When I tell others that I am writing a book about pain and mindfulness, I notice something. They want me to have a conclusion. A quick fix or soundbite that they can relay or remember. I feel kind of sheepish saying "I'm writing this book . . . but the takeaway is really all up to the reader." Most people who received this answer would be polite, because I have people in my life who are masters at playing nice. However, others would have a look in their eyes suggesting I might be wasting their precious time.

Mindfulness is a tricky thing to teach because there is no one-size-fits-all. Pain also fits into this category. Pain is something we can discuss, but we can never understand how it makes someone else feel. Some people are stoic under the worst conditions. Other people may exaggerate minor symptoms.

We don't live in anyone's body but our own.

When we want answers to why we are feeling bad, the world is full of conjecture. We can Google the shit out of anything and prove ourselves correct and incorrect again and again. We can find people in similar enough situations. We can live so much in our heads that it is difficult to take stock of our bodies.

Our bodies are always evolving, always changing. Every week we get an entirely new lining of the gut. Every ten years we get a new skeleton.

We have some tangible examples of the body being an example of transformation. Our fingernails grow, our wounds heal, our hair usually grows back after a terrible haircut. There is no constant (which is great news, because I don't want to be stuck with my haircut from the eighties). Pain stops us. It makes us slow down. It makes us notice this very phenomenon that is occurring all the time. Although it is absolutely terrible to feel pain, it can be the only thing that helps us to remember that we aren't permanent.

These days, we are great at keeping up with the Kardashians, but less great with remembering that we don't get forever in our bodies. Sometimes pain and illness give us a real-life expiration date. Rather than having all the time in the world to get it right, we may realize that we only have years. Why is impermanence an important concept to grasp? It might be because if we realize this, we may stop doing all the things that don't really matter. Being impermanent highlights the stuff that matters. It is like the mattering suddenly has halos and it is just a matter of looking up and seeing those halos, rather than down at the dirt beneath our feet.

See the people who show up and know not to say "I know how you feel." See the meals that show up on your doorstep. See the friends that continue to visit even though you haven't showered and haven't said anything positive to them in months. See when you have less of a need to scroll social media, because #inspiration is much less interesting than flesh and blood inspiration.

When you want answers and you want them now, it is because you have lived so many years in your head. Answers feel solid. Questions feel dangerous. Just for kicks becomes a giant question mark. Try uncertainty. Of course, you can mask your pain with expertise, but it is time to rip off the Band-Aid. Live in your body, even if it's an icky place to be. Let your body heal or let it surrender. While all that you knew before may crumble, there is also a rebuilding happening. Whether you die because of this pain or remain alive, there is a world around you that is trying to make itself known. If you can see what is really there rather than what you want to be there, some of it, I swear, will be good.

All of life seems like it hurts when you hurt. There is no question about that. The answers are not the solution. Mindfulness in action is truly the thing to transform this experience. How do you do this? You start now. You become your questions. You close this book for a moment because it is all about you.

# Mindfulness

## FOR WHEN YOU CAN'T REMEMBER FEELING WELL

When I was growing up, there was a corner store at the end of my street called "Pop's." My sister and I didn't think there was an official "Pop" but we liked to believe it was the patriarch of the family that ran the small store. This store was an important landmark in my childhood. It was where I went with my spare coins from my grandmother or my iced tea stand (I was breaking away from the lemonade trend). It was the first place my mother let me walk alone. I spent what felt like hours looking at the gummy cola bottles and stale caramels, smelling the aroma of candy and magazines. This store started to represent my childhood. When I hit puberty, I was convinced the teenaged cashier was flirting with me at Pop's. (In retrospect, he was just being nice.)

The amazing thing about that store is that it is still there. It is still there, and my parents are still there, on the same street with the same gummy worms. The whole world has changed, but somehow, all those things have stayed steady. Of course, my childhood friends are no longer there. Some have found me on Facebook, arms now covered in tattoos rather than the clothes their mothers picked out for them. Some have drifted into memory, forever seven years old, bossing me around through the foil of GI Joe. I don't like to visit this store as an adult. It just seems wrong to move it into the present day. I don't want to modernize it. I want it to be a feeling, almost more than I want it to be a place.

I thought about my experience with Pop's when I couldn't remember feeling well. It hadn't been that long, maybe six months, that I had been feeling unfamiliar in the land of my body, yet my memory started to map out the new reality and blend it with the old reality. Suddenly, I was "ill" Courtney, rather than just Courtney.

Memory is a tricky thing. We know that pain is a teacher, but it is hard to learn when our teacher spends more time giving quizzes than she does giving wisdom. My memory of Pop's might be inaccurate. Could my pain story be inaccurate, too? One theory is that chronic pain is, at least in part, a memory. The pain-mediated parts of the brain may be calm, but the emotional centers are swirling with activity. When you can't remember feeling well, it can be good to dig into the recesses of your memory. Go as far back as you can in as much detail as you can and remember a time that felt simple. The edges may be fuzzy. You may blend your life with stories you have heard about your life. You may even find yourself living in a photograph that you have seen of your past.

Find a memory where you felt well. Try your best not to "what if" the situation. Just be in a memory and in your new body simultaneously. As you do this, you are helping to release the grip of the parts of your brain that are on hyperdrive, convinced that they have to keep you safe.

*Thanks, hippocampus. You can rest now.*

The hippocampus forms memories, but it also mediates stress. Try to imagine you are moving more into memory, less into stress. Your body is remembering the origin story of your pain and the emotional aspect of that pain every day. Chronic pain can be like an addictive thought. Every day is an opportunity to focus on healing and less on chronic pain memories (but damn, it's hard).

It's never possible to go back, no matter how much we may wish it so. We grow up. Our bodies change. Mindfulness is our chance to grapple with what is, rather than coloring all the time before and all the time after.

# *Mindfulness*

## FOR WHEN YOU CAN'T MOVE FORWARD

If you have become ill or injured, it is so, so normal to get stuck. You didn't plan to become acquainted with this version of yourself, and you might be doing your best to ignore this new person. As a result, even if you are feeling better, you aren't noticing.

I can relate to this. I had a daily routine that looked like a normal morning routine (coffee, dress myself, write, shower, feed my baby) but I was adding in the following:

- Reviewing the origin story of my injury and wondering if I could have done anything differently.
- Forgoing sleep because sleeplessness became so normal that I didn't even question it.
- Cursing every time I tried to put on my socks.
- Forgetting everyone's birthday because I was just too consumed with the discomfort of my body.

My habits were engraining themselves into my brain and, at the time, I didn't realize that they were shaping me into a negative person. Even though I had hundreds of thousands of hours of positivity, this daily routine was making me an expert in the field of down in the dumps.

If you are still with me, don't worry, I'm not going to tell you to circle around three times and throw glitter over your shoulder to make the spell disappear. (Glitter is really hard to get out of carpets.)

Undoing your own negativity is not easy work and it doesn't happen overnight. However, like changing your eating habits, your perspective, or your health, it is worth it.

I am going to assume that you are not liking where you are, and that is a start, but now you have to commit to consistency. If you are going to change something, you need to start doing it today, and tomorrow, and the next day. Your life, after all, is a sum of your habits.

For me, I started working on my sleep. When I woke up after hearing my son move in his sleep my habit was to start thinking, *Oh no! Now I won't be able to get back to sleep. I am going to be exhausted tomorrow. How am I going to get everything done?* In other words, I was freaking out about the future rather than living in the present.

To get myself back to sleep, I started doing something that for me was surprisingly effective. I thought of two things that didn't have any recent stories or emotions attached to them. They might be as dissimilar as butternut squash and hummingbirds, or clouds and cloth napkins. Then, I would let myself keep coming back to those thoughts, the way meditators come back to mantras. There was something so relaxing about this thought process that I often would be able to drift to sleep—and when you can fall back asleep when you don't expect to, it feels pretty amazing.

If for some reason this technique didn't work, I didn't just throw in the towel. I got up the next morning and paid attention. Was I hopelessly overtired? Was I a shell of myself? Sometimes, yes, I was, and I honored that and loved myself anyway. Sometimes a burst of energy came through me and I proved myself more capable than I had realized. I let myself notice rather than forecast. I let myself start a new pattern, rather than continuing to groove doom and gloom into my neural network.

When you can't move forward, just move. Start today, and commit. If you can find the reward behind this new way of being, you will slowly start to strengthen your mind for any challenge. It's that easy . . . and that hard.

# *Mindfulness*

## FOR WHEN NOTHING IS CHEERING YOU UP

There are some things that can almost always put a smile on my face. A cupcake. A yoga class where the main thing I am asked to do is to lie on the floor. A full morning in bed. However, there are times when I go to that yoga class and am just waiting for it to be over, or I buy myself a cupcake and realize it has offered me no pleasure whatsoever.

If you can't glean pleasure from buttercream icing, things are serious.

As a naturally sunny person, it is hard for me to admit that there will be periods of my life where I won't feel like myself, even with all of the pick-me-ups in the world. Recently, I woke up from a bad night of sleep. My body hurt. My soul was tired. I put on something baggy because I had a plugged milk duct from breastfeeding (if you don't know what this is, lucky you). I realized: my body had changed. My wardrobe had changed. What I could do had changed. If I didn't have feelings about this, I wouldn't be fully human.

*Why was I denying myself the experience of feeling badly?*

This is not something we are taught. We are taught to dust ourselves off, to pick ourselves up, to move along. We don't have time for shuffling or stagnation or pauses. That looks like weakness, and worse than showing weakness to the rest of the world is letting our own sweet selves in on that truth.

Since a cupcake was not the answer, I decided to let my sadness speak. I played some sad music. I cried a little. I felt the reality and the weight of the past two years of challenge. While to some, this may be described as wallowing, to me, it was moving through. It was feeling the headache in my frontal lobes, the anxiety in my stomach, the tears just behind my eyeballs. It was ignoring every part of me that wanted to breeze through this experience by focusing on others.

I let the focus be on myself.

Selfish and self-aware are not the same thing. Selfish is also not the same as self-soothing, self-care, or self-compassion.

The cupcake didn't work because it was an outside force. I needed to dig deep within to turn toward my bigger feelings. Rather than labeling my joy as "good" and my pain as "bad" I allowed all of it to be part of the greater collective of who I am.

Life is always in flux. We can't plan our feelings any more than we can plan the way our life progresses. Mindfulness is a way for us to become resilient. The next time you feel that your typical go-to is doing absolutely nothing for you, take the time to recognize that you might be denying that this difficulty is actually happening. Then, take a deep breath and bring the difficulty closer. Invite your tenderness to join you. While you sit within the dark and difficult, remind yourself, "I am here." Create another kind and loving statement to help your body and mind slow down.

Every time you find yourself convincing yourself that the most efficient use of your time is to pour yourself a giant glass of wine and escape into the black hole of the Internet, try focusing within just a few moments longer. Your sympathetic nervous system will be able to function, rather than hiding beneath your okay-ness.

This is not something to do once but throughout your life as you need it. At some point in our lives all of us will need time to self-reflect, but we must remember to remind ourselves, again and again. (Not to assume that I won't have cupcakes in my future. Let's not go overboard.)

# *Mindfulness*

## FOR WHEN YOU FEEL LIKE YOU CAN'T SURVIVE THE PAIN

When I first became injured, I was unable to sleep. I tried to watch YouTube clips, but I couldn't really because I was caught in a dialogue with my body, which was shaking and fighting so hard to rebalance itself. I would lay on the floor with pillows under my pelvis and on either side of me. I was the least uncomfortable I was going to be at that time and still more uncomfortable than I had ever been in my life.

I would get through a day of taking care of my lovely baby with his soft skin and even manage to laugh and smile and feel gratitude. But the night would hit me hard. I would stand in the shower every night, trying to hold onto the sides to balance myself. My legs would almost collapse underneath me. *I can't do this anymore*, I would think. *It is impossible to live this way.*

The most surprising thing about my unbearable pain was that it was, in fact, bearable. I lived another day, I took another step, and some nights I didn't need to sob myself to sleep. I started reading about mindfulness from the perspective of people who had suffered. The old version of me, the one who taught mindfulness, seemed laughable. I couldn't even find her voice if I tried.

When the pain took over my whole body, all I thought was *I can't survive this*. Miraculously, I did survive. Time taught me that the only thing I could ask myself was if I could survive *this moment*. When you are ill or suffering, looking down the path of the future is a long and bleak road. Being in pain is hard and imagining what's ahead is harder. All you can do when things fall apart is ask yourself if you can do it right now. My hope for you is that the answer is yes. Five minutes later you may find yourself with that same voice thinking *I can't do this. I can't survive this pain.* You have to ask yourself; did you just survive it?

Yes.

Do you have any idea what the future will hold when it comes to your body, your healing, or your state of mind?

No.

Predicting the evolution of pain is futile, yet it is where our minds go. Our minds seem designed to worry. It is the deepest layer of ourselves that can do the work of taking a step back and seeing the strength that we no longer feel. Even if our bodies hurt and our emotions envelop us, we can become more and more present to save ourselves from forecasting a life of suffering or clinging to the pleasure of the past. The present is never as dark as we think, nor is it as wonderful. It just is, which sometimes is us lying on the floor, doing our best to fall asleep while pain rips through our body.

Our bodies have changed countless times since they have been born. Every seven years or so, every cell in our bodies is replaced by a new cell. Deepak Chopra said that this is what makes him unafraid of death. He has already done it so many times before.

If your body can manage that, it can certainly survive this.

# *Mindfulness*

## FOR WHEN EVERYTHING SEEMS HARD

I have been awake many times in the middle of the night over the last couple of years. Some nights, I am almost at peace with this. Most nights, I am most certainly not.

Sure, I could be one of those people who use that time efficiently by writing or meditating or warming up some tea. Instead, I use that time to rage and plan. I become angry at elements of my life and angry at the state of sleeplessness itself. Then, I decide I need to plan out my entire life up until retirement. After all, that is the best way to spend a chunk of time at 3 in the morning.

Rage and planning. The nemeses of sleep—and my constant companions.

Planning when you are ill is almost impossible, but, if we are honest (and I'm going to be honest because that's kind of important for this book) many of us do it. We wonder how we are going to accomplish something; anything from tying our shoes to climbing Mount Everest. We wonder how we are going to keep our relationships now that our positivity is faltering. We wonder and wonder. It takes up so much brain space that the brain gives up on the whole sleep idea.

When everything seems hard, it is pretty typical to make things even harder. You're in the trenches, so why not have mud splattered all over you? If this is you, this mindfulness exercise will seem well suited for you. If this is not you, congratulations, you have figured out presence. Your only task is to teach someone else your magic.

When you catch yourself in the train of tormented thoughts (reminder: trademark that name for my future band), it is time to stop searching for the answer. If you are unwell, you may want meaning so badly that you will listen to anything that seems like it could be capitalized. Anything true and real and worth grasping. What is true is the present. Everything else is just conjuncture and speculation. Everything else is your best guess.

When you find your thoughts looking like the following:

*I should look into new apartments because soon, I won't be well enough to walk up the stairs.*

*How will I afford a new apartment?*

*I will have to get another job.*

*Could I work from home?*

*Do I have time?!*

Simply tuck those thoughts away for your future self. I will sometimes think *future Courtney can handle that*, or you may find yourself reminiscing, like I did the other night: *Remember that business trip when I had an obnoxiously comfortable hotel bed? I was so serene in my body. Floating around through life. Unaware. Ignorant. What was I thinking?!*

I will take a deep breath and think *that is for past Courtney*. Past self, future self. Many of our frantic thoughts can be divided into two piles, like laundry that we leave for someone else who actually likes doing it. Your future self is more than competent to handle future problems. You do not have the appropriate résumé, because you are present self. Present self is a little underqualified.

This mindfulness exercise won't make everything that is hard super easy. However, it may have the power to help you fall back asleep.

Future self will take care of it in the morning.

# Mindfulness

## FOR WHEN YOU HAVE TO LEARN FOR YOURSELF

When I was younger (and we're not talking that long ago) I was all about the fitness tests. How long I could hold a plank (which, truth be told, was obnoxiously long). How far I could run. How deep I could push in a yoga pose.

Years ago, I interviewed someone who had been a top yoga teacher. She was one of the rare ones who made a comfortable living through yoga, selling out workshops that were promoted with calm pictures of her body contorting to her will. She was able to do all of the things that people with tight hamstrings (such as myself) coveted. Her face could plant on her shins. She could fold in half at the hip joint as if she were a piece of paper. She didn't even feel many stretches; they were so easy to slide into.

Then, she got severely, horrifically injured. She heard a "pop" and it turned out to be her hip. Things were never the same. Things were so different, in fact, that she turned away from yoga. She made up a whole new way of exercising which celebrated stability over flexibility. She spent time doing things besides always trying to make her body look fitter and better and younger.

I interviewed this woman, wrote an article, and then proceeded to ignore her underlying wisdom. I pushed myself to the brink, and often. A rest day had an underlying thread of guilt. Even when I was pregnant, I moved constantly while my son wriggled around in my belly.

Less than one month after I gave birth, I wore a backpack with a computer in it and wore my baby on the front. No one was watching me, but I was watching me, and damn, I was a tough cookie. Only in retrospect did I realize that I was highly inept at rest. I wanted my newborn to see this strong woman who was capable of anything when really all he needed was my love.

A physical therapist once told me that I was one of the rare patients she had to rein in, rather than tell them to please do more.

Neither one is better.

Finally, I stopped the madness, not because I got wise, but because I got too injured to continue. Then, because I was injured, I started to become wise. I let myself take modifications. I would tell my personal trainer "That's too much for today" rather than pretend that I had no limits, ever. I circled back to the lesson that I could have learned much earlier.

There may be a lesson in all of this pain and discomfort for you. It may not be what you want the lesson to be. It may be hidden under layers of habit. It may be in the corner of your soul, behind the part of you that swears you are just fine. This lesson may whisper, "Please rest," or "Please love me unconditionally," or something else entirely.

Get quiet for a second. The lesson is not going to unveil itself until it feels safe that you are going to stop pushing or acting in exactly the same way you always have. Your lesson is shy and needs your coaxing.

Sometimes we aren't even aware of what we know and what we need until we are still. While you are still, try allowing the whole space of your heart to be flooded with love. With every breath, imagine the love expanding within, to every crevice, to every fingertip. Let your heart feel open to whatever is underneath all this difficulty. Let your heart hurt if it needs to.

May you be happy and able to live in this world with ease.

# *Mindfulness*

## FOR WHEN YOU HAVE A CASE OF THE F$&K-ITS

There is no cure for the common cold. There is, however, a cure for the case of the fuck-its.

My mother despises swearing. It is probably one of her least favorite things on the planet, other than cilantro. I make my living with words and I sometimes like a dose of the swears. When used properly, you can really make your point in a way that "fudge" or "sugar" never will.

Still, I will do my best never to swear in front of my mother (so, Mom, if you are reading this chapter, best to skip ahead).

The fuck-its can happen at any time. They can happen when a migraine triggers a bad mood that lingers well beyond the tension clearing. They can happen when you stub your toe and then realize that exact moment was the highlight of your day. They can happen when you look at your boss and think, "What did I do to deserve your disgust?"

You will know you have this condition when the fuck-its tumble out of you the way a morning person bounds out of bed. You might say it in your head at first: *fuck it*. Then, it might become a mutter, said just loud enough so that someone hears your condition: "*fuck* it." Then, you might decide to share your fuck-its with other people and sprinkle them into conversations. It might seem lighthearted at first, until you start saying it so much that your fuck-its seem like the truth. Fuck it, there is no point of being hopeful. Fuck it, there is no use in trying. Fuck it, your negativity is reinforced again and again and again.

It's easy to stay in this mental loop. Doing something else and trying to remedy our heart pain is so—sorry, Mom—*fucking* difficult.

We start by taking action. We start by refusing to be victims. We start by negating our own negativity. Think of all the things you had hoped to be before "Fuck it" became your mantra. Did you want to be positive? Did you want to be vibrant? Did you want to be more smile, less scowl? Start by saying it is so. As if it is happening right now.

I did a form of mindfulness training known as yoga nidra, and it would start with an intention known as a sankalpa or the commitment we make to support our highest truth. A sankalpa digs down deep into the part of us that needs no fixing, with heartfelt desires expressed like "I am already whole" rather than "I want to be whole." A true sankalpa requires some listening. You may need to sit every day until it arises. It may be the same old intention every single time, or you may surprise yourself. What do you want when you drop all of your facades? State this deep intention in the present. For example, "I am able to see the gifts in my illness."

Whatever is required for you to move forward and to heal and to power through your case of the fuck-its is already within you. You can plant the seed, you can live consciously, and you can see yourself bloom, one sankalpa at a time.

# *Mindfulness*

## FOR WHEN YOU ARE SLOWER THAN YOU CAN REMEMBER BEING

A friend of mine was recently talking to me about her husband finishing his chemotherapy treatments. They were going to be celebrating with a trip; something "normal" from their life before illness. Only, he was different, and she was different, and the pace would be different.

It is hard to be slower. Everything in society extols the benefits of the fast, from express shipping to Internet speeds to the way we contact people (when was the last time you wrote a letter?). If someone says that they are efficient on a job interview, this is considered a positive trait. However, being efficient can sometimes come at the cost of being thorough.

We feel great about ourselves when we get to the end of the day and have accomplished everything we have set out to do. We feel even better when we have lists that are compiled for the very next day. Most of us, realistically, only slow down when we have to. When do we have to? When we are sick. When we are in pain. When our bodies scream out, "*Enough already!*"

When you are slower, take a moment to notice all of the speediness swirling around you. When I was hobbling to the end of my street, I saw past versions of myself: women clad in spandex rushing to exercise classes, men on their phones tripping over the sidewalk or even people in their cars too busy to make a full stop at a stop sign.

Every meditation class has at least one teacher who will say something along the lines of, "Slow down your breath." Doing this can be profound for many people. It can make you notice how fast you were breathing. It can make you notice just how much you needed permission to exhale fully.

A slower pace of life can also make us realize what is in the smaller moments that aren't found when we are streaming one more YouTube clip or getting one more work assignment done. You may notice your neighbors more (and not in a creepy way). You may find yourself listening with avid curiosity. You may notice how beautiful the tree is outside of your window; the same window that has been in front of you for years.

Whether you have the same house, the same family, the same walk to work is irrelevant. Any pain is an immediate shift into a different perspective. One night my partner came back from work and told me about a cranky older man he had encountered. My first thought was, "I wonder if that man was in pain." Pain can make us cranky, and it can also make us compassionate. Pain can make our world physically smaller but emotionally bigger.

Your mindfulness mission is to note what has been presented to you within this difficult circumstance. For me, the easiest one to see was the kindness of friends and even the kindness of students and acquaintances. Very few people made me feel judged. I perhaps felt more love in my life than I ever had before.

Imagine that.

# *Mindfulness*

## FOR WHEN IT'S EVERYONE'S FAULT BUT YOUR OWN

If I made a list of all of the people I blamed for my misfortune, it could be a book in itself. I started by blaming the doctors who didn't hear me, then I moved on to the tired nurses who didn't give me answers. Then, of course, the physiotherapists who misdiagnosed me and worked my body until it felt so much worse. I blamed my partner for not having enough empathy. I blamed my family for not calling enough. I blamed my barista for getting my coffee order wrong. Everyone should've would've could've done it differently . . . and they didn't.

They were obviously terrible people.

It took some—ahem—perspective to realize that my generous sprinkling of blame was not making me feel any better. It was not a healing salve. It just did a good job of stirring up resentment.

In many organized world religions, you need to forgive in order to love more fully. We can't cast people (including ourselves) out of our hearts and expect ourselves to live wholly. The trick is to release the separation and the judgment. The poet Rumi wrote, "Your task is not to seek for love, but merely to seek and find all the barriers within yourself that you have built against it."

Forgiveness seems simple, unless we feel that we actually have something to forgive. Even if you are blaming only yourself, this takes up space inside of you and stands in the way of a good helping of self-love. Blame builds up walls rather than allowing your injury or situation to strip you bare.

If you have dipped your toe in the pool of mindfulness, likely you have been introduced to the body scan. Think of this technique as the forgiveness scan. Ask yourself what, or whom, you need to forgive and sit with that question. We always know the answer if we sit long enough.

As someone or something arises, this is not an expectation to change the situation immediately. It is an invitation for forgiveness to enter. Forgiveness is a lifelong process and a lifelong skill. However, we will come no closer to it if we don't ask ourselves the big, good questions that stand in our way of love and healing. We have to make a commitment to freeing our own hearts.

Our entire life, we get a lot of blatant and subconscious messages telling us to be more interesting and more attractive and more outgoing. We worry about boring people with our troubles. We feel that our own limitations are reinforced though the people who know. We move through life feeling like we are falling short and it is far too easy to get bitter, to get angry, to get even.

I am still working on the process of becoming more Courtney. Not someone who is exceptional at doing everything in a day but someone who can stare out a window aimlessly and feel like enough. I still judge myself when I don't heal in the "right" way. I still hesitate to let myself sit down when I am tired. Find the people who don't see all that is wrong with you and instead see the right. The beautiful people in my life see my enough-ness. This allows me to pattern something new. These people don't need a clean house or for me to put on a nice outfit. They want me, even if I have tear-stained cheeks.

What happens if a mantra was "yes" instead of "no" to all the people at fault, including yourself? Try that mindfulness exercise all day today. The mantra of "yes." We are all trying to find the balance between being enough and being open to more.

# Mindfulness
## FOR WHEN A HUG HURTS

I had a huge fight with my partner after I started living in agony all the time. The worse I felt, the more I felt his distance. He didn't expect to be with this crumpling heap of a woman. He didn't expect to come back from work to someone sobbing on the floor from pain. He went to the gym a lot. He stopped touching me. I felt alone in my body and my relationship.

It was not a great time.

A hug hurt, so he stopped cuddling me. The distance between us grew greater. I didn't realize until I was in pain that the most important thing you can do for someone in pain is to show up and be consistent. A person who is ill has had their world shaken. The one thing they most certainly don't need is shaking.

We pain-dwellers need steadiness.

This bout of suffering occurred right in the middle of the seventh year together with my man. I remember thinking "This is one hell of a seven-year itch."

I believe in the occasional argument in a relationship. Without the occasional release, unsaid words can feel like the beginning of a headache or a kettle just before it boils. Even if it isn't noticeable, it is there, and it may make the rest of a relationship uncomfortable.

So, we fought, and we yelled, and we cried. My man and I argued hard, ultimately about the same thing but from very different angles. I surprised myself with the strength I had within an argument when I felt incredibly weak within my life. We grew tired, and somehow, in the dark of the night, we realized where each other stood. I didn't get hugs, but he did touch my wrist, my hand, my cheek. I realized how healing touch was and how sorely I had missed it.

Even if bear hugs are out the question, find a route to skin-to-skin contact. Even if that feels overwhelming, consider the idea of Reiki, with a hand just above the field of your body. Get connected to the world again through small comforts like physical touch.

Part of mindfulness is knowing yourself, what you need, and expressing that. Like so many parts of mindfulness, this can be easy to say and harder to do. It is why many of us explode like faulty pressure cookers. It is why we blame others when we can't find our own solutions.

If your quality of life has changed substantially, the pain is not necessarily changeable, and your ability to move through the world might not be changeable either, but you can find a new way to express what you need from the world. You may get help from a partner, a friend, a caregiver, or even a paid professional. Your mindful journey starts with you finding a kind place within yourself that will listen to your own vulnerability. It continues when you ask for this without blame or aggression. It finishes when you gain what you need, and you get even an ounce of healing.

I was on the floor because I couldn't get into bed, and one night, I had someone on the floor with me. It didn't stop the fact that I could not sleep. It did stop my racing mind from only thinking *Thissucksthissucksthissucks*. It did give me another breath pattern to focus on. It did allow me to stop my habit of shrinking and retreating and isolating. For a moment, I was more than pain. I was still me and I was still deserving of deep love.

# *Mindfulness*

## FOR WHEN YOU CAN'T DO THE THINGS YOU USED TO DO

Hello, my name is Courtney and I am imperfect. I realize this isn't news to any of you. However, oddly, it was news to me.

I was very lucky in my body for more than thirty-five years. When I wanted it to do something, I trained, and it complied. I sometimes overdid it, but my body would wake up the next morning, sigh, and ask me what I wanted it to do. I was a tough boss. I sometimes gave my body a break through a massage or an acupuncture session, but then I would do yoga in front of the TV, because yoga didn't really count as movement. It was what I did on my rest days.

When I got seriously injured, I was shocked. I kept trying my old tricks, but they weren't working. I was constantly coming to a screeching halt inside myself. *What? I can't tie my shoes? I can't sit at cafés for long times? I can't go to vigorous yoga classes?* I felt terrified. I grasped for control. I cried. I yelled. I rarely smiled (except at my baby, because he could make a blobfish smile. No, that is not a typo, and yes, it is worth Googling. I'll wait.).

I couldn't do the things I used to do, so I stopped being the person I used to be. That seemed to be the agreement I had made with myself. Somehow, I had received the message that doing and being were inextricably linked. In many yoga classes I had taught the concept of human doing versus human being and the fact that we as a society are much better at the "doing" part of life. It made so much sense at the time. And then I got injured.

Things that seem easy (spiritually and emotionally) when you are well, need to be revisited when you feel unwell. The world doesn't make as much sense or fit into any boxes.

And that's okay.

When you can't do the things you used to, it takes time to find the parts of yourself that haven't changed. There are parts of you that have been completely steady, even though you have been through the worst. There are parts of you that are still hopeful and still positive.

Mindfulness involves being patient with time. You can't rush yourself if you are frustrated or angry or going through one of the many millions of steps toward feeling any semblance of inner peace. While you are getting used to what you can't do, take time to give yourself time. When you feel yourself trying to rush the healing process or through an emotion that is crashing into you ("I can't cry—again!"), give it space. Give yourself room to breathe, heal, and feel all of the shitty emotions that come with being a human being going through a hard time.

Notice the language. *Going through* a hard time. Not *living in*. It is more dynamic than any of us think. You might not be the human doer you once were, but you are still one heck of a human being.

O ne recent morning I had a rare chance to sleep in (and these days, sleeping in is 6:30 am). I felt amazing. Therefore, I did what anyone with an extra chunk of free time would do. I scrolled through my phone. *Sigh.* Sometimes I am anything but my best self.

I am certain that you have some version of yourself that understands this. This version of yourself might set the alarm to meditate but then be called back to your warm, warm, bedsheets.

We mean well, don't we?

I used to have the habit of sitting crossed legged anywhere, including on a chair, although sometimes I would drop one leg to the floor and sit with a foot under my caboose. It felt comfortable and it enabled me to maintain good posture. I didn't see a need to change.

When my pelvis went severely out of alignment, all of this torqueing didn't work for me anymore. When I was in my worst pain, unable to sit except for at the very edge of a couch, I would swear that if I felt better, I would never again cross my legs and never again sit twisted.

Time passed. I felt better. And my habits, so deeply ingrained, visited me again. I found myself in the middle of writing an article, sitting in the exact same way as I had prior to my injury.

I am a health and wellness writer, which means I spend my days reminding people in articles of the things I am pretty sure we all know to do. Eat well. Exercise. Stop smoking. Except, we forget. You might mean to eat more plant-based, but you see a cheeseburger and . . . the sizzling meat smells so darn good. You might have every intention for good posture, but . . . you are also tired, and slouching on the couch is just so darn comfortable. You might mean to quit smoking but . . . you get a whiff of a cigarette when you are going for a walk and every cell in your body cries out for it. Our intentions do not always align with our actions. We are probably not ever going to have control of every impulse. The "right thing" will not always win. This is okay.

When you are ignoring the right thing to do, it is because it is easier. Humans default to laziness, and neuroscience (which is probably the least lazy field out there) can prove it. The brain is like your own inner economist, running a cost-benefit analysis. When you give it a choice of pizza or boot camp, what do you think it is going to choose?

Mindfulness relates to the part of ourselves that *realizes* we have been ignoring our best interest. It is the part of us that can take a step back and evaluate. It is the inner grown-up (which shouldn't always win, because inner children are fabulous).

If you need to access the part of you that knows better, you need to sit still. TV and beer and potato chips are all wonderful, temporary ways to relax, but if we require real, honest, powerful transformation, we have to check in. What do you really want from yourself when it comes to your healing? Weigh what would fill your soul in the long run.

# Mindfulness

## FOR PEACE

We like to believe there are diametric opposites in life. Given that, the opposite to pain could be seen as healing. However, I don't believe life is that simple. There is chronic pain. There are hearts that break beyond repair. There is grief that hovers. There are parts of life that we can't recover from. This is not all doom and gloom (although it admittedly sounds pretty gloomy thus far). In the midst of lingering pain there is proof that you love deeply. There is proof that you are a soldier.

There must be an alternative to letting our circumstances embitter us, right? Moving on can't mean erasing all that came before. Therefore, I am going to put peace on the other side of pain. It is achievable for all of us in our own ways, especially when enough time has passed. It is what we can imagine becoming as a result of our turmoil.

Peace is what happens when we start to look at our life from a different angle and when we no longer compare who we were then to who we are now. It is when we make plans that honor our transformation. All of this book's remaining mindfulness exercises give tribute to our passageway to peace.

# Mindfulness

# *Mindfulness*

I am only in my late thirties but I have lived a lot of different lives. I have been a partier. I have been a clean-living yogini. I have been proudly single. I have become a partner and a mother. I have been on a plane every weekend. I have loved staying at home. I have worn heels every single day for years and had other years where I rarely wore shoes.

In Michelle Obama's book *Becoming* she says "I think it's one of the most useless questions an adult can ask a child—What do you want to be when you grow up? As if growing up is finite. As if at some point you become something and that's the end."

We evolve. We change our minds about things. I have changed my mind about relationships, family traditions, soy milk, and bedtime. I have changed my mind about meat, forgiveness, religion, and love.

No biggie, right?

My point is that none of us know our futures. The most we can do is set an attitude that will hopefully guide who we become. Whenever I was in the process of evolving, I would fight an emerging version of myself and cling to who I used to be. There was no greater example of this than when I became a mother. I was so used to seeing myself as someone who was always moving forward, learning, seeing the world, and exploring alone.

Then, I fell so deeply in love with my little son that I could not be that same woman. A new woman emerged, and she was softer in some ways and fiercer in others. This new woman had grit, but she didn't want to explore as much. She wanted to witness. She even wanted to put work on the backburner to place love as her most devoted qualification. It took time for me to accept all of the newness that came with this transformation.

When you have been in pain, you tend to glimpse your future as being one with medications or discomfort. You glimpse a more decrepit version of yourself.

Until one day you don't.

You will know you have turned a corner when you see who you have become as a result of your pain. Likely there are parts that are better. You may be brimming with bigheartedness. You may be more likely to notice a vibrantly orange sunset. You may suddenly speak joyfully about an upcoming vacation, rather than discussing all of the things that you *won't* be able to do.

Life can be fucking hard. There is no way around it. If we live long enough, we will have times when we can't walk the way we want to or be the way we want to. Our journey kicks us in the butt, forcing us to listen and soften and surrender and learn. My ninety-year-old friend wrote to me: "I am pain free for the moment and until the next time it happens. It was a span of two years prior to this [back spasm], so I'm not going to worry about it or else I would never get out of bed in the morning."

If you are mindful, and you live ninety years, you can literally choose not to worry. Until then, when you glimpse a different future, it is time to shed the cocoon of the person you used to be. Feel all the versions of you inside, vying for space in your brain and in your heart. Discard who you aren't anymore, unapologetically. Make space for present you, so that future you can be bolder and even more magnificent.

# *Mindfulness*

## FOR WHEN YOU CAN FINALLY SLEEP

Sleep. It's a beautiful thing, isn't it? Many people don't value sleep until they lose it—or have kids.

When you aren't well, or are worrying about someone who isn't well, something seems to follow the advice of physicians, aunties, and health blogs alike.

Sleep. Motherf-ing sleep.

*You must get sleep to heal!* the world will scream and whisper at you.

*Thanks, well-meaning world. I would if I could* you want to respond. Depending on the type of person you are (or the kind of day you have had) you may answer a well-meaning advice-giver with a graceful "Thanks for your help!"

Or the middle finger. We all have our own personal styles.

When you can finally sleep, it will feel blissful. It may not even be amazing sleep. The first time I felt like I got real sleep, I slept for two hours straight without being woken up by pain. That might not sound like much, but it was glorious.

Then, my sleep increased. I started to have early nights in bed and I treasured them the way I used to treasure dinner parties with people who appreciated the art of drinking and eating far too much. I invested in eye masks. I bought ear plugs. To be honest, I was kind of obsessed with sleep. I would cut conversations short to retreat to my bed. It was my haven. It was my victory.

If you can finally sleep, whether a half hour more than usual or an amount so long someone feels that they should check on you to see if you are okay, it is time to mindfully celebrate. When I really, honestly slept, I felt like I was more myself. A friend of mine who had her own pain experience told me that her doctor saw her before and after an operation and barely recognized her afterward. She seemed like an entirely different person, because uncomfortable, poorly slept people are not the kindest or best looking. I understood this viscerally.

Mark any improvement with this meditation. Sit or lie down or hang from the ceiling. Just breathe. Then, focus more on what is going right than what is going wrong. Just for a moment. It may be just the sleep. That's okay. Focus on the rightness of that. Breathe. Every time that well-trained negative mind wants you to listen to it, try to circle back to what is right. Just for now, this is your task. Without figuring out how to optimize your wellness or reflecting on past crappiness, let yourself focus on this one point of your real self.

Deepak Chopra recounted a meditation retreat where he didn't wear shoes. His feet, unaccustomed to the hard ground, became sore. His meditation teacher reminded him that the foot lifting away from the concrete felt incredibly good. "Focus on that," he suggested.

It's all about perspective. Our pain is loud but there are other sensations in you that can keep you grounded. There is no need to ignore your full experience, but it is worth exploring your unique expression of joy.

# *Mindfulness*

## FOR WHEN YOU CAN IMAGINE GETTING BETTER

*Dear Stomach Knots,*

*Thank you so much for your concern. You have given your ample time convincing me that things would not be okay. You were a valuable asset to my emotional team. However, in the coming months, I will not be needing you on a full-time basis. This in no way diminishes my respect for you—you have certainly kept me safe and you know well how to make yourself heard. However, I am looking to reconfigure my team.*

*Respectfully yours,*
*Courtney*

When you aren't well, you aren't only stuck with an ill body. You get a whole host of other visitors, from toxic thought patterns to inner feelings that feel as physical as the illness. This can also happen in reverse, for if your mind isn't well, your body may hop on board. Your heart may feel broken for the life that you will have trouble living. Your stomach may be churning, trying desperately to get control.

When you are sick, you often have more time to yourself. Whether it is because you can't move as much as you used to or because your tendency is to say no to plans, it is hard to be in the world in the exact same way as before. Your definition of getting better may change. It may mean seeing your old sense of humor in this brand-new body. It may mean reconnecting with the you that isn't obsessed with your pain; the part that has the capacity to laugh uproariously with a friend, even if your bones and soul hurt.

I noticed I was "getting better" when I didn't grimace the whole day. When I could ask my partner how his day was instead of regaling him with the difficulties of my own. Some of this was physical improvement, sure, but the majority was emotional. I started waking up and reminding myself what I was grateful for. The first time I started this practice, my mind was dripping with sarcasm. *Oh, sure, I'm sooo grateful for a cup of coffee . . . I can't walk!*

That's why so much of mindfulness is in the practicing, because it isn't easy to stand up to life's challenges and to insist that you can live differently in spite of them. If your thought patterns are all pain, all discomfort, all the time, it can be hard to get out of them. Notice what is good, even if it is a minuscule moment in a full day. Notice the purring cat beside you. Notice the get-well card from someone you love dearly. At the end of the day, before you rest, can you remember anything at all that wasn't horrible?

There must be *something*.

When you can imagine getting better, even in your mind, you have done the work. The work will not happen overnight, but when you have a day when you smile, laugh, and feel more yourself, you deserve to soak it in with every atom of your body.

The good, the bad, the ugly. You are the only one who gets to witness all of these things in your life firsthand. When you move through the ugly and see a little good embedded in it, well, you have found the magic.

# Mindfulness

## FOR WHEN YOU REMEMBER
## WHO YOU ARE (AND WHO YOU WERE)

When I lived in Switzerland, I had an apartment that overlooked the Alps. Except on incredibly foggy mornings, I started my day with a homemade latte and a view of snowcapped mountains.

Many apartments in Switzerland have a particular "look" to them. They have small fridges built into the cabinetry. They have toilets that flush with a giant button on the wall. They have induction stoves that require a particular cleaner in case of any burn marks on the surface.

The Swiss are fastidiously clean, and you *don't* want burn marks on the surface.

For four years, I scrubbed my stove with this cleaner, then I moved back to North America and found myself mostly with gas stoves. I remembered a lot about Switzerland, such as the outgoing expat community that held me up and the Sprüngli chocolates I took home with me every Friday evening.

I forgot about the stove.

This story is not to help you remember all of the cleaning products of yore, but to help you recognize that we don't keep everything in the front of our memories. Things move into the recesses of our minds. Our minds get into grooves, which yogis call the Samskaras. I always agreed with this philosophy that we lean into thought patterns, whether consciously or unconsciously.

I realized that having a "new" old memory was a good sign. I was remembering who I was. I was remembering where I came from. I was looking beyond sensation and lack of movement and seeing the little moments that made me who I am today.

For a long time, I thought fit and healthy were the defining terms of who I was. I got up at the crack of dawn to exercise. I ate salads in mixing bowls. I hydrated like a boss. Then, I was injured and unfit and different. I kept desiring to crawl back into my old identity, not realizing that one of the gifts of being in pain all the time is that I could remember I was more than my body. I was more than my ability to be physically strong. I was more complex than I could have imagined.

On the days when you realize that you are more than your pain, you are experiencing great healing. You are working yourself into a different groove. You are connecting the dots between who you were and who you are, which is a lot more circuitous than obvious.

If you need a boost, phone or email an old friend who knew you when. Ask for a memory from when you spent lots of time together. Chances are, it will be vastly different from what you remember. It will give you a window into a world when you can marry your past with your present. Take a moment to witness what this reminiscing does for your body. Do your shoulders drop? Does your breathing change? Or are you still gripping?

Nothing is wrong or right. You are not in the mindful journey to manufacture joy. You are merely in this to be more authentically you.

# *Mindfulness*
## FOR WHEN YOU DO SOMETHING MIRACULOUS

I f you have practiced meditation, have you ever had a session where there was not one single thought in your head?

Of course not.

Sometimes we expect the impossible when it comes to meditation. This is a perfect microcosm of the rest of our lives. It can be hard to function when we are trying to live up to our own perfectionism. Mindfulness and meditation are not about being perfect. Far from it.

Your healing journey doesn't only have to be celebrated when you feel like you have completed the restoration process. There is a giant spectrum of well and unwell, and even moving slightly more to the well side is worth noticing. Observing the gradients is part of mindfulness, and it can keep you from feeling like a very different version of yourself, or, allow me to be blunt: feeling like crap.

What may be miraculous will change from week to week, month to month, year to year. The first miraculous thing I did was have a shower without leaning on the wall. The second miraculous thing I did was walk to the corner (with help, a lot of stops, and pain). The third miraculous thing I did was put on my socks without extreme struggle. These milestones are months and years apart. They are all extraordinary.

Whatever miraculous thing you have noticed is worth sitting with and praising. (Any time I write sitting with, I don't mean physically sitting, by the way. In a book about discomfort, you are the best teacher of what position will work for you.) You may have washed your hair. You may have held a pen and had enough energy to write a letter. You may have simply listened to someone without a hint of comparison.

Just breathe, slowly and deeply. As you notice your pain and discomfort, think *Oh, there you are.* You are acknowledging that pain is with you, but at the same time you are acknowledging that it hasn't *become* you. Your pain or discomfort might keep coming back. Let it know that you hear it, so it won't feel like it has to keep reminding you of its presence.

*There you are. I hear you.*

Whatever part of you has even 1/100 of healing, bring your attention there. Imagine the space that is now there. Imagine you can continue to send a stream of healing energy in that space. This meditation can be a minute long on a hard day, or significantly longer on an easier one. Brighten your day, regardless of the status of the sunshine outside of your window. Recalibrate your view, little by little.

# *Mindfulness*

## FOR WHEN YOU START TO FORGET THE PAIN

I'm writing this from bed, because I'm having one of those days where every time I get a chance to lie down, I lie down. (You know that you are having a lazy day when your senior aged cat is more active than you are.) As I rest and nap and refuse to push, I realize that my pain taught me so many things. When I'm tired, I rest. That is a revelation. When my workout involves more walking than burpees, I am grateful for the opportunity to move.

These days, I don't seem to have much patience for people who don't appreciate their functioning bodies. You know the type—the ones who can do the splits but bemoan that they can't do a handstand. The ones who run a marathon but sigh because they didn't hit their PR. In other words, I am impatient with who I used to be.

People. It is time to get grateful.

Like so many things in life, we need to learn firsthand from our bodies. If we didn't, we could just collect our parents' and grandparents' stories and sift through what was relevant and inhabit their truth. Instead, too many of us need to be stopped by injury or illness to *get it*. Then *it* becomes clear. *It* makes sense.

If you are one of the lucky ones, your pain starts to slide away. You may find yourself feeling something you forgot how to feel: normal. When you start to forget the pain, you may take for granted the fact that it is now easy to get out of a chair or to stay awake or to talk about something else. You may catch yourself acting like your body is not as fragile as an eggshell.

Theologian, philosopher, and mystic Meister Eckhart is quoted as saying "If the only prayer you ever say is thank you, that will be enough." Whether you are in communion with acceptance or you are feeling a physical difference, practicing gratitude will help unlock the parts of you that have clenched ever since you got the pain signal. I went to the dentist after I had been struggling. The hygienist asked me "Do you typically grind your teeth?"

I wanted to say, "No, not typically, but define typical after a challenging year." Instead, I more succinctly said "No" because it's challenging at the best of times to get a word out at the dentist's office. Apparently, my whole body was tightening in anticipation of more pain.

Our minds are incredibly good at sifting through all of our memories to draw comparisons and to find examples of all the ways pain has occurred. *See?* Your mind likes to tell you. *Every moment before this one was leading to this moment!* Your mind means well. It is trying to keep you safe. It is also incredibly taxing—and inaccurate. Our memories distort over time. When we start to forget the pain, this is a reminder that there is a mental way out from the suffering that we have gotten really good at.

When my pain became a little less, this was the first time I could imagine doing a body scan. A body scan when you are shaking on the floor is not a good idea. A body scan when you are in mental anguish is also not fantastic. When I was in one of my worst states, I went to a restorative yoga class. I cried through the whole thing, especially when the teacher said "Relax in any position that feels comfortable."

*That doesn't exist, perfectly able-bodied lady in spandex,* I thought.

When I started to feel moments of release many months later, I started the process of making friends with my body. I scanned through it and said hello to all of the parts that I had neglected. If you are feeling a smidge better, try to sit and remember. Remember your neck, your face, your jaw. Remember your shoulders, your ankles, your inner organs.

*Thank you thank you thank you.*

In the midst of all you have been though, this body of yours, remarkably, has given you more days. Your body has continued to work. It worked even when you didn't want it to. It worked when you didn't even have a shred of faith of it.

The gift of pain is in the ability to see and be grateful for what is right in front of you. When I came into pain and then out of it again, I was able to realize how remarkable it was that I could get out of bed, that I could stand up, that I could embrace someone.

*Thank you thank you thank you.*

# *Mindfulness*

There was probably a time in life when you can remember not being in pain, or even not being in *as much* pain. Your pain-free days may seem like very long ago. This is not surprising, because pain can create a tunnel and the world outside that tunnel may seem like it is steadily moving away from you.

I had an evolution of pain for over a year. It started with my back, but it was a whole host of things that came along with being a new mother. I got mastitis on my birthday, on Christmas, yet I still doggedly breastfed. One painful night, I realized that I was so determined to breastfeed because I wanted to feel that I could do something, anything, on my own terms. Keeping another human alive was something I could be proud of, no matter what other changes I was currently resisting. I was so stubborn that this breastfeeding insistence affected how I experienced pain. I couldn't take a lot of drugs because they would be shared with my baby. I remained miserable and incapacitated and a heck of a lot of fun to be around.

When someone came over or tried to call during this period, two things happened:

1. I ignored their attempts to contact me.
2. I told them my pain story.

I am at a stage in life where I have very little ability to bullshit. Some people call this their thirties. I can certainly talk around a truth if I need to, but if I am asked directly, I will tell you how I am, even if it is not hunky-dory. My pain story was relayed and retold and through my own version of broken telephone became something entirely different. Life before became smaller and life after became, well, everything.

One day I told a different story. This different story was by no means remarkable. It was a story about how I made soup. I make really great soup, if I do say so myself, and it had been awhile since I had had the stamina to stand in the kitchen and stir a pot. For months I could only cook in two-minute increments before I would have to take recovery time to sit down and catch my breath from the hurt.

This time I made a whole pot of soup.

Captivated yet?

Of course not. To you, this is a very basic human function and a very boring story. To me, the pain sufferer, it was everything. I not only made the soup; I told the story of the soup.

The days when your life transforms dramatically do not exactly *feel* dramatic. They feel like little twists on the every day. This is where mindfulness can be helpful. Mindfulness doesn't ask for the bold. It doesn't ask you to heal overnight and lecture at TED Talks. (Although that would be cool and here's hoping.) Mindfulness asks you to be so attuned to your life that you notice when you tell a brand-new story. It asks you not to expect the sensational, but to find life in itself sensational. Little bitty moments are what will ultimately transform you. Tiny soup stories are what refuse to give pain your whole heart and soul.

*That* story, the one other than your pain story, is what healing is all about. It may not happen today, but in you is your very own soup-making story. Yes, you too can be that interesting.

# *Mindfulness*

## FOR WHEN YOU CAN LAUGH AGAIN

The other day, my partner told me that nothing on the planet feels like making our son laugh. So many parents have said exactly the same thing because parenting is filled with clichés that only make sense when you meet your kid. Children's laughter is unabashed. It is free of shame and doesn't need much wit. On some days with my son, I make as many fart sounds as I use language. He finds this as funny as a Netflix comedy special.

It is great for my self-esteem.

It is only when you laugh for the first time after something difficult that you realize you have had a hiatus from laughing. The first laugh feels odd, the way speaking after a silent meditation retreat feels. There is a jaggedness and hoarseness to the laughter, as if your body is figuring out how to respond to the sound.

You are always a new version of yourself after something difficult. Not only are you composed of brand-new cells, but you also have new wiring in your brain. Laughter needs to find its place amongst all this newness. While before you might have chuckled at pratfalls, now you may wonder how the person's body feels after. While you might have liked a racy joke, now it may seem crude.

You have changed. Your laughter needs to find its voice.

The first time I laughed after my injury, it hurt. It hurt my whole body. I screamed *stop!* to the offensive humorist, who took my juxtaposition the same way people take those same words from someone who is being tickled. Yes, I was laughing, but I needed to ease my way into the experience. My body was only ready for a little at a time.

I don't need to tell you to notice your first laugh after the storm. This will be surprising to you, and surprising things are the things that we remember. However, you can try to notice how laughing may alleviate some of your emotional stress. Laughter can be some of your complementary medicine on this part of your healing journey, like acupuncture. It is not your cure, but it is a darn good practitioner.

Go on a spiritual quest for the funny. Funny TV. Funny people. Funny yoga classes (laughter yoga is not for everyone—including me—but it may work for you!). Guffaw. Chortle. Shriek. Get comfortable in the language of merriment. Dip your toe in the water or jump in butt first. Exercise your diaphragm and jog your inner organs. When we laugh at a joke, we are mindfulness in motion.

# *Mindfulness*
## FOR WHEN YOU CAN DO SOMETHING SIMPLE

It is so easy to minimize progress. In fact, it is the norm. See if any of these conversations sound familiar:

"You look great!"

"Thanks, I lost five pounds!"

"That's amazing!"

"Yup . . . just twenty more and I will be at my goal."

\* \* \*

"How are you feeling?"

"Oh, you know, okay. I'm still recovering, but I can now open jars."

"That's great!"

"I still have so far to go."

Notice how the response to "That's amazing" or "That's great" is an undermining of the experience as well as a reference to the long journey ahead? The journey ahead, as long as we are alive, is just going to keep unfolding. We may get out of pain or discomfort, but then something else will happen to us down the road. We may lose the weight, but then need to put some back on for our health in the future. Now is not then. If we don't spend any time at all in gratitude, we are going to miss all of the good stuff. It took me more than six months to even notice that I was minimizing. I got back the feeling in my legs, but I was so darn stiff I couldn't move. I then could move, but I was so darn inflexible. I gained back some flexibility, but . . .

The buts were standing in the way of seeing how far I had come. I couldn't get out of bed for a long time, but I eventually moved myself into a world where I could stand and walk without pain. In the quest for a perfect, pain-free body, I wasn't noticing the miracle of the body I am in.

The simple thing that your body can do right now that it couldn't do last month is proof of miracles. It flies in the face of every negative thought you had. It defies the people who didn't believe you would get better. It is grace's way of saying, "See? I'm still here! Just stop for a second and *pay attention*."

If you find yourself hearing a loud sound without bracing after experiencing a traumatic event, or taking a bite of food when you haven't been able to stomach anything, or any of millions of possible advancing acts, *stop*. You are on a quest for full and complete healing, but *this* moment matters.

I am going to make the assumption that you are busy, and don't have any time to spare. Center yourself anyway. Prove yourself wrong. Close your eyes. You have a mantra to repeat at least ten times slowly:

"I am grateful for _____."

Fill in that blank with whatever this new simple act has given you, or you can just silently repeat "I am grateful for healing."

It's happening. It may not be on your timeline or agenda but the practice of gratitude will help you realize that you aren't moving backward. Life propels you forward, even in the most challenging of times. When it comes down to it, life is much more challenging and much more beautiful than I could have imagined.

Let's end those conversations differently.

"That's amazing!"

"It is, isn't it?"

# *Mindfulness*

## FOR WHEN TODAY IS BETTER THAN YESTERDAY

Even people who are pain free have great days and horrible days. This reality doesn't make most of us feel any better or any less alone when we are in a funk. I only seem to be aware of dark clouds over my head once they have lifted. I not only become nicer, but everyone around me seems nicer. I no longer contemplate living on an island by myself, encouraging my misery with margaritas. (Although I will rarely turn down a margarita.)

When my mood starts to lift, I can see more clearly. This doesn't take all the struggle away. On more than one occasion, my pain has been sneaky enough to recede, giving me confidence before returning to take over my body. Sometimes the pain returns full throttle and sometimes it merely niggles. It jumps out of my relaxed body the way masked people do in haunted houses. Just like a haunted house does, my pain returning scares the bejesus out of me. I no longer feel safe. I'm not sure what to do, so I walk around with my shoulders hunched and my body shuffling. My face contorts and cringes.

I can remember one specific instance when the pain decided to camp out, but I was tired of giving it all the power. That was the first day I had a today that was better than yesterday. I had a conversation with my sister about how most of us acquire phenomenal coping skills, until we go through something that is too darn difficult to use those coping skills. Then, we have two things to accomplish:

1. Throw out the old coping skills.
2. Start fresh.

This is *very* hard to do, which is why when we are in the throes of pain or misfortune, we say things like: "I worry that I am going to be like this forever" or "I don't know how I will ever get through this experience." Most of the hard experiences of our lives don't last forever. Most don't even last a substantially long time in the scheme of life. Yet that is where the mind tends to go (although it rarely seems to go that way when we are on an island, margarita in hand).

We have to train ourselves to get through today.

I used to have an evening routine of pain relief. I would take pills upon pills. I would rub my back with arnica gel. I would have a hot shower. I would put a hot pad on my back and do my physical therapy. I would have my last cry of the day. When I got to the end of it, I would think, "There. I did it."

Sometimes getting through today is enough.

When we can experience any today, whether it is streaked with tears or reasonably easy, we can start to see progress. Maybe today is a little better than yesterday because you feel slightly less sorry for yourself. Or maybe you were surprised by a fit of laughter (which happened to me recently when my partner told me about a goat yoga class where the goats wear diapers. I could not get that image out of my head.). Anything that makes today better than yesterday is progress. It is you looking your pain in the eye and saying "I see you, but you will not rule me."

Start right now. What are you doing? You are reading, of course. But what else is there? What emotions, what thoughts, what plans, what awareness? Can you "just" read and let the rest go?

Doing one thing can be much harder than doing many things. There will be moments in your pain journey when you will desperately want to escape. However, there will also be times that you will interrupt your own happiness out of habit. That is a poor habit we all have and one we all have to conquer. Try to take a breath, read a book, or have a conversation. Drop the rest, even just for a moment. Only then will you be able to see the "real" today in front of you.

# Mindfulness

## FOR WHEN YOU REALIZE WHAT IS IMPORTANT

I was in an Uber the other day when someone cut off my driver. Rather than getting irate, he chuckled. "I guess *someone* is important," he said. Those words stuck with me. I think we all fall into importance traps. It is why we check our work email even though we could take the day off to be with our families. It is why we half listen to conversations while making lists of things that only we can get done.

I haven't worked for a company since 2010, and with me as my own boss, I can run into mountains of self-importance. These moments happen to all of us when we think we are different from everyone around us. When we are the only one that gets "it." (And, man, there are a lot of "its.")

I read recently about a *Top Chef* contestant who passed away at the age of twenty-nine. She was down to earth in a way that my extra decade had not yet accomplished. Fatima Ali penned an essay about her terminal cancer for Bon Appétit magazine. "I am desperate to overload my senses in the coming months," she wrote, "making reservations at the world's best restaurants, reaching out to past lovers and friends, and smothering my family, giving them the time that I so selfishly guarded before."

She died three months later.

We get glimpses of our own mortality, and in these glimpses, we vow to become better. We get clear on the things that matter. We refuse to waste our lives away. Illness, sickness, and pain can be so consuming that we might fail to see the underlying gift of life. (Shocking, I know.) Our pain lets us know that no matter how much yoga we do, or how much water we drink, our bodies won't always cooperate. Our bodies are limited. You could wallow, or you could let this recognition be the fuel for all the things you could be doing.

Which bucket list items will this pain allow you to start?

If you, like Fatima Ali, were given one year, what would you do differently? If this pain continued and your life forever altered, what solace could you provide yourself? What time are you selfishly guarding that you could share with someone else?

When I am caught up in the streams of negative thinking, I try to get myself out. Even on my worst days, I must remind myself that there are podcasts. There are lattes. There are cozy bathrobes that get cozier with time. There are cookbooks to read. There are friends to call. There is a hand to hold. There are things that this pain has not taken away from you, and dare I say it, there are even things this pain has given you. What is important when there isn't work and your own importance standing in the way?

Get a piece of paper. Make a list. And get started.

# *Mindfulness*
## FOR WHEN PEOPLE DON'T SEE YOU ARE IN PAIN

There is no ideal way for someone to support you. Your partner might feel protective, while to you their behavior comes off as overbearing. Your loved ones may give you space, while in your mind it feels like they are deserting you. Your spouse may come up with new solutions or treatments and it feels like they just aren't listening. It is hard to be in pain and it is hard to be with someone in pain. How can you get perspective when you are overcome by sensation or mental struggle?

The person who is closest to you is not experiencing what you are experiencing. They will never. Fully. Get. It. My partner gave a lecture the other week about back pain that was comprised of a lot of phenomenal images: CT scans, radiographs, MRIs, and the like. It was a great presentation. When it was over, I thought "Wow. Even up close, you can't see the pain." Some of these people had the most severe pathologies but very few symptoms. Other people had spines that looked near perfect but symptoms that were debilitating.

Doctors can't see it. Your partner can't see it. When it feels like no one on the planet "gets" you, you either complain more in the hope of people understanding or shut up because you don't see the point of communication. The first has the same effect of speaking your language louder in an attempt to get a foreigner to understand. The latter has the same effect of drifting off to sea all alone on a paddleboat built for two.

There will be some people that get it, but the majority will not. Everyone is engaged with the thousands of thoughts running through their own heads each day. Pain is part of the communication system that tells us we are in danger. When we feel endangered all the time, there is no way we are going to act normal. Even though you don't feel normal on the inside, people may see the same old you, eating mushroom Bolognese and getting sauce on your shirt. (Guilty.)

One of my dear friends suffers from depression. She sometimes will cease all forms of communication, including responding to texts. I am as guilty as anyone else of getting caught up in my life and forgetting to send her "I love you" texts with no expectation of reciprocation. I am guilty for refusing to see the silence for what it really is, until the moment has passed.

Consider this the "cutting people a break" mindfulness exercise. It is a break for the people in your life who mean well but say the wrong thing. (A friend who was going through IVF treatments told me someone said to her "But it was *so* easy for me to get pregnant!") It is a break for those people who have tried to make you better, but you're not better, and they have run out of things to say.

Think of it as the loving-kindness meditation. Start by thinking of three people who are large forces in your life: people who might visit you at the hospital or hear you cry or even say the wrong thing most of the time. Then, think to yourself: Thank you for supporting me. May your life be healthy and filled with ease. Try to feel the support of the ground beneath you or the chair you are sitting on. Try to feel the support of that person and imagine, for now, that they mean well.

We can spend a lot of our energy feeling angry for how people are or aren't reacting to us. This can take a lot of our reserves, but let's be honest: you need every ounce of your vital forces to dedicate to your healing.

# Mindfulness

## FOR WHEN YOU CAN BREATHE AGAIN

*I will never be able to breathe normally again.* That is what I told myself one night when every single breath hurt. We breathe, at the minimum, 17,000 breaths a day, so that is a lot of hurt. Turns out, I was wrong. There have been a lot of nevers in my life, but I find myself declaring them less and less as I get older. Here are some I have been completely and utterly wrong about.

*I will never forgive that person.* (Years passed, and I got tired of my anger. Forgiveness arose because of the sheer exhaustion of holding onto resentment.)

*I will never be a stay-at-home mom.* (I enrolled my kid in a daycare, then pulled out at the last minute. I didn't want to miss a second of his young childhood.)

*I will never live in suburbia.* (My partner likes to declare that we are too close to downtown to be in suburbia, but I am in a house and I cook my family's dinner most nights. It counts.)

*I will never stop partying.* (I did. I gave a long, hard fight to the end but now I can hardly hold my liquor and I like an early bedtime.)

All of the "nevers" we tell ourselves are making one assumption: things will stay the same. More specifically, nevers are based on the hypothesis that *we* are going to stay the same. This is why getting older helps us from making blanket statements. Once we have enough experience in our memory banks, we know that life is anything but predictable and that we can be wrong.

Even about ourselves.

When you find yourself in the midst of healing, you may have to retract some of your nevers. I will never be able to walk again? *Look at me walking!* I will never be able to socialize normally again? *Look at me wanting to go out!* I will never be able to dance all night again? Well, maybe some things still hold true.

Your mindfulness practice allows you to notice when you were wrong. This is not to keep a scorecard so that you can train for your career as a perfectionist. This is to give yourself the benefit of the doubt. This is to make you realize that your negative thoughts are just that—thoughts. They are not reality. They are feelings and fears and mental representations, but they aren't the truth.

Buddhists describe the mind as a monkey, meaning that it chaotically swings from one branch to the next. (In all my years, I have not seen a chill monkey, but never say never.) Acknowledging that our brains are like this is a way to help us understand that the negative thoughts may be something we focus on, but it is also possible to distance ourselves from them. Note that I said *possible.* Not easy. (Mindfulness is not simple. Did I mention that?)

You may have to make a practice, every single day, to fine-tune your awareness of the way your brain works. Formally, this is meditation, but it can also be seen as putting your monkey in obedience school. It will help you from catastrophizing or overgeneralizing. It will help to stop those nevers. When I paused—which for me might happen in the middle of a hot shower rather than on a mediation cushion—I would hear myself say "I will never breathe again." The pausing would give me the space to think to myself "Well, maybe you are wrong." Imagine if you were wrong about all or even some of your negative thinking patterns. What would be possible?

# *Mindfulness*

## FOR WHEN YOU FEEL YOURSELF RELAX

You may not be out of pain now, or maybe ever. (Way to start a chapter, Courtney. I swear, I'm going somewhere with this.) Even so, you can shift and no longer live in anger and fear. You can unclench your tight fists and find ways to live life with an open hand.

It is so hard, for all of us, to rest back into what is uncomfortable. It is much easier to stay in our comfort zones and in our patterns. It is much easier to coast through life, staying up to date on weather patterns and finding inventive ways to eat the crumbs at the bottom of a bag of chips. (One idea: snip off the bottom corner and let the chip dust fall into your mouth. I may be a health coach, but I am not a wasteful woman.)

One image that is particularly poignant during times of meditation is waves. Waves show up in many relaxing environments: vacations, spa waiting rooms, or the wall of a yoga studio. Even though the crashing of water on rock can be deafening, it also can be remarkably soothing. Up-and-down waves can be a metaphor for the up-and-down moments of our lives. Up-and-down waves can match the up-and-down nature of the inhale and exhale. Up-and-down waves can remind us that pain, even when it stays, doesn't stay steady. It ebbs, and it flows. It sits at the forefront, then it recedes. As we begin to recognize this, we can move away from our own obsession with ourselves. Working with pain or discomfort or heartache requires tenderness. As we begin to relax, we can raise our gazes away from our navels to see who happens to be just like us.

The isolation of pain can be incredibly introverted work. It is unlikely that you feel like corresponding with others or being in the world when you are learning how to cope with words like throbbing, stabbing, aching, or agonizing. When you feel even 1 percent more relaxed, you can bring an intentionality to your mindfulness practice. You can do a "just like me" meditation. Whatever you are doing, imagine all of the other people in the world doing it, too. For example,

Breathing in and out, so are others, just like me.

Doing the dishes, so are others, just like me.

Lying on the floor, so are others, just like me. Crying in the bathtub, so are others, just like me.

Mindfulness can be a way of turning inward, but eventually, it helps us regain awareness. We are not living alone on Pain Island.

Then, bring a giant wave through your body. Imagine it crashing within you, rising and falling. If it helps, put on the soundtrack of the ocean. As you relax you can let others in and maybe, just maybe, you can let some light in, too.

# *Mindfulness*
## FOR WHEN YOU HAVE PERSPECTIVE

One of my best friends and I were talking about her father who was in palliative care and going through the five stages of grief for his own life. He spent a lot of time in denial, especially because, for a time, he didn't feel much pain. Drugs are a wonderful thing, but they also keep us from realizing that we are mortal. In case you haven't recently brushed up on your stages of grief, they are denial, anger, bargaining, depression, and acceptance. In other words, they are the cheat sheet for most of our pain journeys.

Most of us have no interest in aligning with our pain. We want to get as far away from pain as humanly possible. We want to show it the door. However, my wise friend informed me that one of the most important things she learned from her father's cancer is that you have to get on board.

The title of this book might make someone who was in the denial phase look for other things to read. However, once you are through denial, once you have fought your own challenges, once you have bargained for a better body, once you have sat in your own depression, you might, possibly, enter a space that looks something like acceptance.

Within the space of acceptance, you may have aligned with your body. This is very different from going to a yoga class and noticing your breath for a few moments and then walking out and badmouthing your boss on the way back to the office. This is a longer-lasting union. In the acceptance phase, you and your body are no longer two separate forces, combatting one another. You guys might even be buddies.

Raise the white flag of surrender. It is time to move forward.

Perspective can arise when you are no longer dividing yourself. Although it may feel empowering when you aren't accepting an unfortunate reality, it can make your nervous system kick and scream to get you to listen. In response, you might enter a cycle to try to ignore said kicking and screaming (which, as anyone with a toddler knows, is not an easy thing to do). You can numb with drugs, with isolation, with chocolate cake, with control.

I teach mindfulness and have perspective on my pain not because I am holier-than-thou, but because I started stressing out young. I would freak out if I got less than an A on an assignment. I would sweat before work presentations. I would rehearse travel in my mind (and generally, the rehearsals were not pretty).

It. Was. Exhausting.

Mindfulness allowed me to see what was worth freaking out over, and what wasn't, which truly is most things. I still fall into the trap of anxiety from time to time, because it is deeply rooted and well taught. However, I also notice that it is just that: a pattern.

I doubt there is anyone on the planet in severe discomfort who didn't have any of the five stages of grief. I doubt there is anyone who skipped the hard stuff and went straight to inner peace. That stuff is *earned,* friends.

How do you get perspective? You start by noticing. How do you habitually react? How do you draw yourself away from aligning with the truth? How do you react to any less-than-perfect news? Knowing yourself is not as simple as it seems. You change in miniature every day. You only notice when years have passed, and the miniature has become colossal. Then, if you get stuck with deep pain or trauma, your eyes become accustomed to noticing the colossal.

You need glasses to see the small print on the eye chart of life. We need to retrace steps to see those miniature letters. We need to be still to catch the perspective. There is no shortcut. I did a simple exercise this week that may work for you. I waited until I felt the need to fill some space. We all have these moments: the ones in which we watch the next episode or text the next contact on our phone. I saw this space and I forced myself to take it like a woman, with everything that was captured inside of it. In that one fillable space, there was fear and boredom and the need to control. There was physical discomfort and mental struggle.

An easy acronym for this experience is STOP. S for Stop, T for take a breath, O for observe, and P for proceed consciously. STOP-ing in this way can help us release our addictions to our smartphones and our nightly desserts. It can be scary but revelatory. We need to give ourselves the chance to STOP to gain the strength that will get us through the hardest moments of our lives. This doesn't mean that you won't die or that you won't continue to hurt. It does mean that you will find moments where you can remain an empty vessel. You don't have to be filled, or fixed, or made better. You can be vulnerable and quiet and maybe, just maybe, learn to live with courage and with purpose. Use this mindfulness exercise to help you recognize that you are enough.

# *Mindfulness*

## FOR WHEN YOU FIND SOMEONE WHO UNDERSTANDS

*E*xactly.

That was the word we were looking for when I took my Wellness Coaching training at the Mayo Clinic. We practiced listening intently to a person; rephrasing what was said. We then waited. Pausing can give you a lot. People start talking more. What might have been a short story would be elaborated. It was like magic. People would say things like, "That's *exactly* it."

Being listened to and being heard makes people feel fulfilled in a way that few other things can. You stop interjecting your own experience and instead let the person tell you what they feel and who they are. Just because I am writing this does not mean that I am flawless at this practice. Far from it. I get super excited about commonality and have a habit of talking about my day before I ask about someone else's. However, I am getting better, mindful moment by mindful moment.

That's all any of us can do.

When I was on the floor, unable to move, incapacitated, I was lucky enough to have fingers that still worked. I started typing. I contacted people who said they could help me. I got to a point where I was willing to drain my savings for a breath of positivity or for a new perspective. It was during one of these digital searches that I met a woman in California who worked with people with extreme back pain. Her expertise was born out of her own spinal misfortunes. Her work was a form of coaching and a form of personal training. I immediately signed up for a short free session with her and she made me feel hopeful and capable, two things I had not felt in a long while. She then gave me the email address of a man who had been through almost exactly the same experience. The same inability to sit, to stand, to sleep. Someone who had started the process of getting better without surgery. I emailed him immediately.

This kind stranger wrote me back his story within days. It was to the point and it wasn't sugarcoated. He told me what had helped him, and it wasn't only the obvious. It was trusting in the process and in his body. It was guarding against the pain less and having more faith. It was working for him. He was golfing. He found freedom. He encouraged me, a woman he never met, with the words "Stay positive and don't let the pain take away from the joys in your life. Smile and laugh as much as you can and if you're having a bad day with the pain, just remember it's temporary." He gave me more than anyone did at that moment.

When you are sick, you don't need a thousand people to "get" you, nor do you need hundreds of sympathy cards. You need one person to listen. You need another to understand. The journey of finding those people is undeniably regenerating.

Let me assign some mindfulness homework for anyone suffering in any way: feel understood. Find your person. They may not be in your friend group or your city or your country, but the world is connected, and you can bet there is someone who has cried parallel tears. When you have found this person, the best gift you can give them is to listen back. You can stop your running thoughts to hear what this person is grappling with, because even after healing ends, life throws curveballs.

You will know that you have mindfully listened when you can remember what has been said to you. You can keep the listening going by nodding or typing back a question ("I would love to hear more about . . . would you mind sharing?"). Imagine listening with your heart as much as with your ears. When you are feeling cynical, this process can sprout hope.

Who knew email could be so powerful?

# *Mindfulness*

## FOR WHEN SMILING BECOMES THE NORM RATHER THAN THE EXCEPTION

I was known as "smiley" as a teenager. The funny thing was, I was trying very hard not to have this distressing moniker. I wore a lot of black. I listened to "alternative" nineties grunge. I slouched.

The corners of my mouth always turned up, betraying me.

I didn't have a chance.

Years later, I taught yoga at a senior assisted living apartment complex. Eighty-year-old-plus bright-eyed ladies came in with canes and walkers, ready to meditate with me—the overly smiley yoga teacher. We started the class with conversation and every week there was a host of aches and pains that my young mind could not even fathom. I couldn't relate because I was fifty years younger, so I listened. And I smiled.

When I myself became badly injured, I thought of these ladies. I could understand them instinctively. I gave silent props to them for their smiles in the midst of bodies that were struggling to move down the corridor. I respected them in an entirely different way. It is one thing to get your butt out the door and onto a yoga mat when you are young. It is quite another to shuffle and smile when you are over eighty. Trust me. The elderly are badasses.

These women chose to make the best out of where they were in a building that was in desperate need of a coat of paint. They rejoiced over snacks and tea. One woman came every week with a full face of makeup. Newly inspired by my past students, I decided to stop being a sour puss.

Did I succeed every day? Hell, no. However, my decision to smile was heartening. It allowed me to believe that "smiley," the person, was somewhere in there and that all I needed to do was go searching with a flashlight and some hope.

Eventually, I became a smiler again.

I still had setbacks. I still had stiffness. I still got sick, had bad days, or just simply was in a bad mood. But I saw that there was light in life even when things were tricky. I had role models that were fifty years my senior who were battling their way through friends dying and bodies betraying them. I could choose to etch more worry lines on my face or I could start getting better grooves with the smile lines that were already there.

Here's a silly little meditation to try when you are tired of the grump. Do a big, fat, fake smile. The kind of smile you plaster on when you are standing beside someone you don't really like but have to pretend that you do like.

Got it? Good.

Then, think to yourself, "My mouth is smiling." Mindfully, let the smile spread. Maybe it will get to your chin and cheeks. Maybe you can start to feel your whole head smile. Maybe the smily-ness can spread to your entire body (but that's pretty advanced stuff). Then, give it away. Spread it to everyone you love and everyone you don't. Imagine everyone being filled by the energy of this one smile. One smile can lead to another. One tough day can lead to a good day. We can't predict where this pain will take us, but we can determine the essence of who we are.

# *Mindfulness*

## FOR WHEN YOU BECOME THE EXAMPLE

"Wherever you are, be there. If you can be fully present
now, you'll know what it means to live."
—Steve Goodier

As much as the word "influencer" might be thrown around these days, it is hard to emotionally handle being an example. It is much easier to fade into the background, because once you are held to anyone's high standard besides your own, you feel a great deal of pressure to keep up appearances.

No matter how you may look or feel or how many pushups you can do, things will change. We live in an image driven world; so much so that if you are inept with a camera it feels like a skill you have to acquire. Long gone are the days when you would develop photos to find few that weren't fuzzy or obstructed by a thumb. Now it is all about good angles and proper lighting. Even a bowl of oatmeal has been elevated when it comes to Instagram accounts.

We may wish the world to believe that we are doing well, but in the same vein, we wish that people could see below the surface. There are hashtags that hint at such things, but most people don't like to read more than 280 characters.

Becoming the example is wonderful, but it is also dangerous. It doesn't allow for evolution. It asks us to stay in our glory, when glory, like everything else, fades and mutates.

People want to hear the healing stories. I felt like I heard a lot more from people when I was doing better, because it is much easier to hear that than to hear the opposite. We don't have words to reply to something along the lines of, "Actually . . . I'm doing worse." Worse is not a space that we like to enter. It is much easier to brush off the difficult with false promises. "You're on your way . . . I just know it!" people may nervously chirp, hoping that you will go back to being easier to be with. Anything to move the conversation along.

This is not to say that there is no space for gratitude if you have suddenly and unexpectedly become the example. If people are now holding you to a standard of healing, or even sending people in your direction to spread the good word, it is worth pausing in amazement. Look how far you have come.

Yet this is also a time for honesty. What is the point of pain if not to make you more glaringly honest? You are the example and it is time to own more of who you are. Yes, this moment will change, but where you are right now is what someone is hoping and praying for. You can let people know that you aren't only expecting upward trajectory, but nor are you only expecting downward trajectory. You have arrived in the present moment.

Whoa.

The best gift that you can give someone who is looking at you on your pedestal is the present moment. Remind anyone of where you are, and it will give them permission to be where they are. This is true even if you are on the island of joy and they are on the continent of sorrow.

You no longer have the need to cover up pain or be trite with your words. You can powerfully admit when things are fabulous and when they are bullshit. We have enough preaching going around us. As an example, it is your duty to live your present truth.

# *Mindfulness*

A dequate. Suitable. Settled.

The above three words were ones that I actively avoided. When people would ask my travel-loving partner and me when we were going to "settle down" we would answer "Never." The term "settle" was one thing, but "down"? It wasn't exactly the elevated language we were hoping would direct our lives.

We train ourselves for the difficult situations during the easy times. Attitude becomes a habit, so when I found myself in the midst of difficulty, I did what I had always done, and I tried to rise above it. I refused to join pain acceptance groups because of the very term. No way in hell was I going to accept that this was *my* body.

People love a fighter. They love hearing that you are going to "beat this." No one wants to hear "I've accepted where I am." It feels defeatist.

To make everyone else feel better, we may continue the inner fight for a long time. It is how we condition ourselves to do well in life and to bounce back. The unfortunate reality is that pushing through doesn't always work. Life doesn't always need knock-down, drag-out fighting.

Sometimes all our bodies need is for us to accept and surrender.

This can be a lot harder than doing *something*. It took me a long time to realize that accepting did not mean giving up. It meant softening. It meant having a day where my jaw wasn't clenched the entire time.

Data suggests that greater acceptance of chronic pain is associated with fewer pain-related difficulties. If we avoid the reality of a difficult situation, the pain barrier expands until it is hitting us in the face, yelling "Will you listen now?" We need to find meaning in life, even if ongoing pain is part of our story. We need to find what is valuable in the midst of what is burdensome.

Here is an exercise. Notice when you are trying your best not to accept something. You may be grappling with a whole host of denial; from the language you use when speaking about your condition to the way you treat your body if it feels broken. (I told a friend when I was at my worst that I felt broken and she said, "You're not broken. You're just healing." Language matters.)

Then feel what is underneath the lack of acceptance. Is it sadness? Is it fear? Is it anger? Is it all of these things?

Give each of these emotions time to breathe. Sadness might need more space. Anger might need to roam free. When you stop telling yourself that you "should" be feeling anything, you give your real emotions a chance to explore. When they aren't confined, they tend to take up less space than you think they might need. Rather than having house guests who are always hanging out in your kitchen, these guests may merely need space in the garage.

Sick and suffering people are often told that they should be feeling grateful. "You're alive!" well-meaning optimists chirp.

What if you aren't feeling grateful?

We have to stop covering what's real with a happy face. It sucks to be sick. It feels even worse when we feel pressure to be aggressively positive. Your pain needs room inside of you, and when you stop denying it, you may be surprised to discover that it doesn't require the entire residence of your body. It may need its own room, its own suite (for the fancy emotions), or its own corner. When you invite your truest feelings in, when you accept that this is where you are, there may in fact be room to open other doors to hope.

# *Mindfulness*

## FOR WHEN YOU STOP WONDERING WHEN THE OTHER SHOE IS GOING TO DROP

Growth and evolution are usually very gradual in our lives. They are something we only notice in retrospect. One night I was home alone, watching my son's face on the baby monitor, and trying to fall asleep. My back was starting to hurt again even though I had enjoyed a few pain-free months. As I turned off my reading light, I felt waves of panic, fear, and distress come upon me.

Spilling over with emotion was not what surprised me. It was the fact that I let my remorse wash over me, and then I let it go. I even got a good night's sleep, because how better to deal with a body that is struggling than to rest?

The next morning, I thought "Huh." The "huhs" are also known as the "ahas" but they are a little quieter. They are the growth markers.

I wasn't going to move forward through my life assuming that everything was going to turn out perfectly, but I was also no longer stressing out that I only had so many months of comfort.

"You can go to crazy town. Just don't build your house there," advises grief consultant Karen Milsap. I love this advice. When we let ourselves go to crazy town, we can unlock some of the tension that accompanies discomfort, pain, and yes, grief.

It is equally important to leave crazy town.

People from the outside may see that you are feeling better, or you just have found the correct filter on Instagram to insist on your top-notch-ness. There is, however, an aftershock of pain, even if the pain subsides or disappears. Pain leaves us with an element of shock and disbelief. It requires time for you to heal emotionally, even when the emergent agony has receded. It is natural to need time to be authentic while you wait for life to throw you another curveball.

Life might indeed throw you another curveball right when you are in the middle of that healing process, in which case, you will need more mending and more time. If it does not, you may get a glimpse of the version of yourself that can exist when you aren't wondering when the other shoe is going to drop.

Quick etymology lesson: this expression apparently came from the super small apartment buildings of the late nineteenth and early twentieth centuries. One would hear their upstairs neighbor take off a shoe when they arrived home. Where there is one shoe, there is almost always another, creating an expectation to hear the same sound.

English lexicon history aside, when you have unexpected silence in your life, you can reflect on how far you have come. Perhaps you have managed to live more moments in the present rather than reflecting on your past misfortunes. Perhaps you have had a down-fall, but it didn't destroy you emotionally.

Mindfulness reminds us that sorrow shifts, as does great joy. The hard work is to sit with your own unique flood of thoughts as often as you can, noticing them and letting them go. The overwhelming thoughts eventually are given no more weight than what you are going to make for dinner. (Although my dinner plans admittedly do take up a lot of space in my brain.)

The German philosopher Arthur Schopenhauer once said "The first forty years of life give us the text, the next thirty supply the commentary." As I inch toward forty, I am hoping for a life that intermingles both. I want a lot of text. Moving through my pain is one way to attempt this.

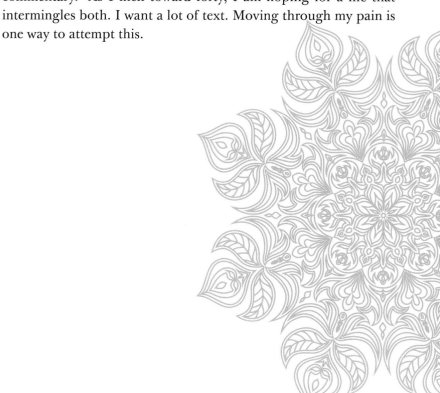

# *Mindfulness*

## FOR WHEN YOU SEE A BEAUTIFUL DAY

Some days in life are inarguably wonderful. The birds chirp and the snow melts . . . unless you like snow, in which case, it billows like frosting on a cupcake.

This is *your* wonderful, after all.

On these sorts of days, people smile at you in droves and of course you grin back.

How long has it been since you have felt like that?

Pain can exhaust you to the bone and it can change everything around you, including the cupcake snow. Smiles become scowls and sunshine becomes too hot. The long list of things you have to be grateful for dwindles.

Most of us fear pain and loss of autonomy. When the thing you fear comes to pass, it makes you different. Sometimes you find ways to cope and to make peace with the change. Sometimes you become bitter and crotchety, even when you aren't in an age bracket that warrants crotchety.

The most beautiful days are the ones that we can notice *in spite* of the frustration and the rubble that has been left in the aftermath of our difficulty. It is astounding, to ourselves most of all, when we can see that we still have precious moments bursting with abundance.

Suddenly, and maybe only for a moment, we aren't comparing our suffering to that of others and we can just be happy. Or even happy-ish.

For a long time, I not only was unable to see my beautiful days, but I was also blind to the beautiful days of others. I didn't listen to their stories of joy because I was stuck in what I perceived was true, human difficulty.

There is no doubt about it: being in pain is genuinely awful. We are caught between the self who felt free and this new person who is trapped. It is much easier to pretend that this dichotomy doesn't exist and slink into easy distractions like television, the Internet, and brooding. (Brooding can be a full-time hobby. Trust me.)

When I was a kid, I was a champion daydreamer. When I took a break from daydreaming, I would bury my nose in a book. I didn't look up much. Mind you, I had a lovely childhood with two parents who raised me to think I was great. However, I also had a school experience that taught me to believe (at the time) that my avid enthusiasm was not so great. I was bullied. Children don't have the language for intense emotional experiences. Without language, they find different coping mechanisms. For me, it was books and daydreams, two portals to my future career as a writer. As an adult, I had language, but in pain, I still desired an escape. My head and my body were worn out. Once again, I stopped looking up.

I missed the sunsets and my partner's kind eyes. I missed the cozy blanket that sits on top of my couch. I missed the tap in my home that dispenses boiling water, making a cup of tea a breeze. I missed everything besides my baby, because he was too cute to pass up.

I read articles and I wrote emails. I watched great shows. I found solace in some of it, but I was also missing the beautiful that surrounded me.

To see your beautiful day, you have to start by opening your eyes and averting them from whatever is your favorite, tried-and-true distraction. Your task is to find something beautiful around you. It may be the scent of a lemon, the stars in the sky, ice cream in your freezer, the leggings on your body, the hug of your dog.

It is there. Find the beautiful. On bad days, even one thing will be a stretch because your mind just won't be in that space, but on good days, you may find yourself having trouble keeping up with all the beautiful.

There are so many moments where I am with my son and I can't capture the amazing on camera. He laughs as he hides behind a baby gate. He throws himself into my arms for a hug. He understands a word for the very first time as if I can hear his brain go "click." The amazing parenting moments happen quickly, and they happen all the time.

My son gives me glimpses into the beautiful day that is always being had, whether I can walk briskly or sit in agony. In the movie *Life Itself* there is a quote that gave me chills. "Life brings you to your knees. It brings you lower than you think you can go. But if you stand back and move forward, if you go just a little farther, you will always find love." Where is your beautiful?

# *Mindfulness*

The other day I took a bad picture. A *really* bad picture.

On the list of things that matter, this ranks very, very low. Emotionally, I know this, but my brain doesn't always register an enlightened attitude. The picture made me look older, serious, and like someone I didn't know. I was not a fan of this woman, yet I couldn't scrub the image of her from my mind. I am not even someone who looks in the mirror often, but suddenly, I was thinking about my looks. A lot. The trivial was taking over my thoughts.

No matter how self-aware you are, you have had moments when the trivial takes up far more space than it should. As an example, my partner has a thing for humidifiers. Stay with me. He wants them to be filled and running and it truly, truly matters to him. I try to get on board, but to me, they are just humidifiers. (Sorry, babe.) Sometimes I am convinced he loves those humidifiers more than he loves me. (On some days, he probably does.)

The point is, we can all get a little skewed when it comes to our priorities. (Again, sorry honey, your humidifiers are awesome.) When it comes to pain and discomfort, this is even more possible. You stub your toe and it hurts, then your toe stops throbbing, but your attitude continues to throb. You become emotionally hurt *because* you physically hurt.

Getting seriously hurt or uncomfortable is a slap to the ego, and the ego doesn't do so well with being slapped. (To be fair, who does?) The ego might respond by becoming haughty. How dare your body betray you like this? You are too superior of a person to have this be *your* body!

The ego is really freaking good at taking up all the space in the room so it may be hard to hear anything else, including your own healing. Clinging to the trivial, to the body you used to love, can have you miss the body you have now.

When you notice your progress, it *is* progress. It is when you notice that your back may be stiff, but you can take the dishes from the dishwasher with a little less discomfort. It is when you notice that your whole body is aching, but you were able to be civil to your sister-in-law. (Score one for being the bigger person!) It is when you notice that your muscles are beginning to relax simply because they aren't bracing for the next blow.

Our culture is set up to reward perfectionism. We reward only the highest caliber athletes and earners. We compliment only the youthful. We pay attention to the miraculous rather than the hard work. We don't leave room for the subtle.

When healing is slow, it can feel like it isn't happening at all.

The progress *is* there, even if it is itty bitty. Your mindfulness journey—a body scan here and there—will give you information. The body has an enormous capacity to heal, but if it is abused with negative thoughts, it can be extremely hard for it to remain healthy.

Rest. Repair. Regenerate. Every minuscule piece of progress needs your attention to get to the next level. Focusing on the trivial and waiting for perfection can make the whole process whiz by. You don't want to miss the good stuff. Not the perfect stuff, but the good stuff.

A meditation I "liked" to do when I was at my worst (in quotations because, honestly, I didn't like much of anything when I was suffering) was to imagine a healing light coming from the crown of my head. I imagined it warming and bathing all the way through my body. Some days, there would be dark zones where I couldn't bring the light in. Other days, I was more successful. As with all meditation, I did my best not to expect anything, nor to judge myself for my reactions. These check-ins were moments when I could just be. Being is what gives us information about exactly where we are at.

What has changed in your body and in your mind since you have felt uncomfortable? Do you need to be perfect to feel healed? I'm sure you have heard "don't let perfect be the enemy of the good." What if you are "good" right now? Not great, but good? Bad pictures, new body, and all.

# GLOSSARY OF TERMS

## BODY SCAN

This is a type of meditation where the meditator focuses on the part of the body being "scanned" through visualization. Some body scans work on penetrating and relaxing the point of focus, while others ask you just to pay attention to one point at a time (for example, your shoulders). The body scan is a great introduction to body awareness and a way to drop beyond the thinking mind.

## MANTRA

Very simply put (and I am interested in making the esoteric simple), mantras are a statement repeated frequently, on purpose. They could be inspired by the fictional *Saturday Night Live* character Stuart Smalley: "I'm good enough, smart enough, and doggone it, people like me." Or a mantra can be a single word: "Peace." "Relax." Traditionally, a mantra is repeated in Sanskrit in order to be considered a sacred utterance.

## MEDITATION

This is a more formal type of mindfulness. Consider it training to help you from getting in your own way of being mindful. How many times do you intend to be mindful but get distracted? (Sorry, what was I writing? There was a really cute cat video on *Ellen* . . .) Meditation can encapsulate all sorts of different techniques, from breathing practices to mantras to visualizations. It is intentional and often involves sitting still. Think of meditation as your formal practice and your mindfulness practice as your business casual practice.

## METTA MEDITATION

This Buddhist meditation is a way to cultivate our inner kindness. It involves mentally sending goodwill to those outside of yourself (and toward yourself too), becoming more inclusive with your feelings of love and tenderness.

## MINDFULNESS

I've always liked Jon Kabat Zinn's definition: "Paying attention; on purpose, in the present moment, and non-judgmentally." Non-judgmentally encapsulates the acceptance or peace we might be working toward in the difficult times of our lives. There is no "right" or "wrong" way to feel in mindfulness. You can do it in all sorts of different situations, but I don't need to tell you that. You have a whole book on that subject. *Ahem.*

## PAIN

I am defining pain as the suffering that comes alongside, or even within the aftermath of illness or injury. I believe that the pain behind emotional trauma can be as damaging as the more scientifically minded definition of tissue damage.

## PEACE

Tranquility and a sense of being at ease with your circumstances, no matter what they happen to be. American Tibetan Buddhist and author Pema Chodron writes, "To stay with that shakiness—to stay with a broken heart, with a rumbling stomach, with the feeling of hopelessness and wanting to get revenge—that is the path of true awakening." That is where peace starts to hatch.

## PERSPECTIVE

I took an art perspective class that showed me how objects appear to get closer together the farther away they are from an object. It also showed me a different way of looking at the world. Perspective is our lens, our way of considering something. Our individual perspectives are shaped by our up-to-the-moment beliefs and experiences.

## SANKALPA

This is a rough definition, as the word sankalpa can have more than six definitions in Hinduism, Sanskrit, and Marathi. The way I use this term is limited but I refer to it as a heartfelt desire or conscious intention. In Sanskrit, "san" means "a connection with the highest truth" and kalpa means "vow." A sankalpa is often said in the affirmative rather than being another "I want" or "I need" sentence.

## SELF-CARE

Something that almost none of us tend to do unless we are burnt out, exhausted, or ill. Self-care is filling your own cup, preserving your (emotional/mental/physical) health and self-initiated wellness. I would go as far to say that it is always mindful.

## YOGA NIDRA

Yoga sleep (my type of yoga) is a meditation technique that is guided. You lie down the whole time and ideally remain fully conscious (although you aren't doing it "wrong" if you fall asleep). There are a bunch of stages that may include intention setting, body awareness, breath awareness, visualization, and, of course, "waking up" (the worst part, in my opinion).

# ACKNOWLEDGMENTS

I never thought I would write one book, let alone two. I had always hoped and dreamed, but dreams don't always come true, no matter what Jiminy Cricket says.

Thanks to all of the people who support my dreams to sit in front of a computer and imagine.

Thanks to all of the people I know who see value in self-improvement, self-reflection, and patience.

Special thanks to . . .

Nicole Mele, who saw the promise of a book in the midst of one of the most challenging periods of my life.

Suzanne Sunday, for her willingness to evolve and for her deep well of affection.

Suchot Sunday, for teaching me how to play the piano and many other things I have forgotten. Will never forget your big sister love.

Joseph Sunday, for always showing up exactly when he is needed and demonstrating the satisfaction that can come from a good dose of quiet.

Carrie Hojnoski, for being the most quotable woman I know and for being such an amazing friend, mother, and human.

The women in my life that make me stronger just by knowing you, even when we don't talk. Just knowing that you exist makes me smile: Carolina, Carla, Heather, Meghan, Sofie, Berta, Emily, Vanessa, Sen, Cheryl, Gaineil, Katy, Vandana, Donna, Annie, Monica, Sarah, Maria Laura, Helena, Waverley.

Stephen Cook, for being resilient and at peace with life's biggest challenges.

Hutton Alexander, for being an example of class, humor, and friendship.

Aniela Gorecki, for being a revolutionary thinker while raising one heck of a family. You are deeply missed.

Michael Jurkiewicz, for showing our boy the best version of what it means to be a man and for having so much love in your heart. (And your credentials are awesome, too.)

Theodore Sunday, for allowing me to see the capacity of the world to love and for inspiring me to do the hard work every day.